Scent
and
Soul

The Extraordinary
Power of the Sense of Smell

Rohanna Goodwin Smith

Scent and Soul: The Extraordinary Power of the Sense of Smell
Copyright © 2021 by Rohanna Goodwin Smith

scentandsoul@telus.net

In some cases, to preserve anonymity, the names of persons and places have been changed.

Author Headshot: Chelsea Minatsis

Prominence Publishing

www.prominencepublishing.com

Scent and Soul: The Extraordinary Power of the Sense of Smell / Rohanna Goodwin Smith. – 1st ed.

ISBN: 978-1-988925-80-6

For Maren and Charlotte
May you always revel in the aromas of nature.

Table of Contents

Part One

Fragrant Beginnings

My father was a master craftsman whose sideline was scent. Standing at his baking table, he would spin magic with his ingredients while the delicacies already birthing in his ovens exhaled their tantalizing aromas. With long fat wooden paddles, he would withdraw the racks of plump, sweet-scented loaves of bread, golden-crusted apple pies laced with cinnamon, savoury cheese and onion tea biscuits and my favourite—butter tarts oozing golden syrupy strands of sugar and vanilla. Each item contributed to the bakery's fragrant mélange.

Dad's refined olfaction was the secret to his successful modus operandi. When supplies were delivered to the back door of his shop, his nose delved deeply into crates of butter, eggs, cream, and tubs of seasonings and condiments. All were assessed for quality and freshness. Even at home when he opened a packet of peanuts or pretzels or uncapped a bottle of beer, he sniffed and judged before indulging. And prior to lighting his evening cigar, he'd run his nose along its entire length before grunting his approval.

As I wandered through the bakeshop as a child, trying my best to keep my hands out of trouble and not get in the way, I was dwarfed by giant mixing bowls that whipped cream into billowy peaks and churned icing into gloppy mounds. Strawberry, rhubarb and cherry pie fillings bubbled in kettles and teased my tastebuds. My ultimate destination was the monstrous mass of puffed-up bread dough that stretched across Dad's baking table. I barely cleared the height of that enormous table, but when I was invited to punch down the dough, I enjoyed my power as it hissed and sank. Afterward, Dad would hand me a warm butter tart and I'd hug his apron-covered legs, releasing clouds of flour into the air.

I chose not to follow my father's profession to become a baker and left behind the safe, fragrant bosom of his bakeshop to enter the rewarding though the oft malodorous career of nursing. But I had inherited his penchant for sniffing his way through life, and my hunger for enticing aromas was satisfied by frequent visits to the perfume counters of posh department stores. Seduced by the latest offerings of Guerlain, Chanel and Dior, I rewarded myself following graduation from nursing school by fleeing to Paris. While inhaling the city's charms, I strolled its cobbled streets and dipped crisp, buttery croissants into frothy cafés au lait at every opportunity. But the highlight of that visit was slipping into the city's ornate, legendary perfume houses, which offered my nostrils a utopia of scent. As I familiarized myself with the language of fragrance—sillage, nuance, top, heart and base notes—I never dreamed that one day I would be creating my own perfumes.

Following Paris, I was lured by flower power to the patchouli-drenched streets of San Francisco and lotion-scented beaches of Los Angeles. Canadian nurses were welcomed with open arms and high salaries in California in those days and I flourished in that milieu, basking on the edge of new trends and radical thinking. I did it all—stretched in yoga class alongside long-haired hippies, loitered in the aisles of incense-laden bookstores, explored numerous spiritual paths, studied astrology and became a vegetarian.

Meanwhile, subtle changes were occurring in my smell preferences. The earthy odours of health food stores, the West Coast's briny sea air and later the rural aromas in verdant Marin County satisfied my senses and usurped any desire to loiter in the perfume aisles of department stores. But I recall as though it were yesterday squeezing my way into the tiny, crowded outlet of the original Body Shop in Berkeley in the early 1970s. The store had been converted from an old garage. Simple wooden shelves held vats of bio-degradable lotions, shampoos and bubble baths, which the staff would custom-scent before pouring them into refillable plastic containers. The concept for the company, along with its casual, low-key ambiance and the philosophy that supported the nascent trend of caring for the planet, was unconventional. But it became wildly successful, and other shops like it sprouted up across the US. However, a similar business with the same name was also operating in England, and in 1987, after intense negotiation, the Berkeley owners sold their business name to the UK firm for a windfall of three-and-a-half million dollars—big money at the time.

The movement initiated by the Body Shop, which encouraged simple packaging, recycling and becoming better citizens of Gaia, felt right, and I supported it wholeheartedly. At that time, the conversation regarding the nature of the ingredients in commercial body care products and perfumes was only beginning. The secrets of the trade remained in the domain of chemists in mega cosmetic and fragrance companies. As consumers, we remained blissfully ignorant.

It was another fifteen years before my personal relationship with smell was profoundly altered. Standing in a small health food store on Canada's West Coast, I uncorked a tiny, unassuming brown vial, sniffed its contents and experienced an olfactory epiphany. Never had I been so deeply affected by an aroma. It stirred within me the memory of some primal beauty of a bygone era when a more direct, intimate connection with nature existed. A time before humankind had been lulled to sleep by ever-increasing isolation from the natural world and its replacement with artificial substitutes. I had inhaled the essential oil of lavender, a powerful, herbaceous floral with benefits so numerous and far-ranging it was to become my holy grail of essential oils.

That brief, captivating whiff remains lodged in my memory as one of those pivotal moments in life when one is redirected without expectation. As a result of that experience, I committed to the study of aromatherapy, the new and popular health modality that was scenting its way across the seas from Europe to North America. Reveling in the beauty of aromatic botanicals entrusted to our planet by Mother Nature, I embarked upon a new career path—the marriage of scent and healing—as if it was a calling.

Lavender
Lavendula officinalis

Botanical Family:	*Lamiacea*
Country of Origin:	France, England, Tasmania, Bulgaria, Croatia
Fragrance Group:	Top note
Aroma:	Herbaceous balsamic floral
Extraction Process:	Steam distillation
Derived From:	Flowering tops
Valuable Uses:	Physical: antiseptic, cuts, insect bites, inflammation, burns, sunburn, aches and pains, spasm, cramps, hormonal imbalance
	Emotional/Mental/Spiritual: anxiety, shock, nervous tension, insomnia, emotional imbalance; comforting, nurturing
Of Added Interest:	Dubbed the "Swiss Army Knife" of essential oils, lavender benefits mind, body and spirit equally. It enhances the action of other essential oils.
Contraindications:	None known

The Mystery of Smell

From scents sublime to odours foul and noxious, smell penetrates deeply, affecting us in conscious and unconscious ways. Powerful and unavoidable, it is the only sense over which humans have little, if any, control. To live, we must breathe, and with each breath—approximately 24,000 per day—odour molecules register in the brain without our conscious awareness or permission. The unexpected arrival of an aroma—fleeting though it may be—can connect us to our fondest memories, deepest longings and buried fears, and in doing so may influence our physiology, psychology, sexuality and spirituality. The importance of smell to our overall health and well-being can't be underestimated. And so it has been since the beginning of time.

Olfactory Evolution

With noses on alert, our earliest ancestors foraged for food and ferreted for mates. As they made their way across foreign landscapes, a keen sense of smell was crucial to their survival. Odours, brimming with information, were not only invitations to nearby food sources; they also signaled danger, were a connection with kin, an indicator of health, a carrier of joy and a conduit to the divine.

Yet smell hasn't always remained on equal footing in the hierarchy of the senses. Three centuries ago, the Enlightenment, also known as the Age of Reason, spread throughout Europe and characterized a new worldview. By encouraging independent thought and freedom of expression, this movement led to the belief that the faculties of intellect and reason reigned supreme. Scientists and philosophers alike viewed sight and hearing as the intellectual senses, and many of them considered smell too ethereal or, conversely, too animalistic, vulgar and base. With its connections to the past, smell had no place in civilized society, particularly since it was believed its relationship to emotions might prompt a lack of self-control. Until the early twentieth century, scientists had postulated that, when man ascended to an upright position, his olfactory organs had begun to shrink and that the sense of smell was surely destined to atrophy over time with the advancement of civilization. Famed nineteenth-century perfumer G. W. Septimus Piesse held more lofty aspirations for the sense of smell. In *The Art of Perfumery*, he wrote:

> Of our five senses, that of smelling has been treated with comparative indifference. However, as knowledge progresses, the various faculties with which the Creator has thought proper in his wisdom to endow man will become developed, and the faculty of smelling will meet with its share of tuition as well as sight, hearing, touch, and taste. [1]

Smell Makes a Comeback

According to modern biologists, although smell may be the most primitive of our five senses, it may also be the most sophisticated. In fact, olfactory research—presently at an all-time high—has determined that the olfactory bulb is twelve percent *larger* than it was in our early predecessors, affirming—in my opinion—smell's ongoing necessity and value. Since embarking upon the study of aromatics, I've cultivated a renewed respect for the powerful anatomical instrument mounted in the middle of my face, and I marvel at the physiology of olfaction. For example, before I savour the first sip of my morning dark roast, millions of excited sensory neurons in my olfactory bulb have picked up the odour molecules. This bulb—a small portion of brain nestled behind my eyes and sitting high up in my nose—acts as a relay system for transporting odours from the external environment to the area in the brain where they will be interpreted. Neurologist and smell researcher Dr. Alan Hirsch suggests we have an invisible universe at the tip of our noses, impacting everything we do.

Yet scientists appear to know more about the mysteries of the universe than they do about the intricate workings of the sophisticated system of olfaction, and until the turn of the twenty-first century, they had remained baffled as to how the sense of smell actually functions. It was 2004 before the first Nobel Prize ever awarded for olfactory research was presented to two smell scientists, Linda Buck and Richard Axel, for their theory about how the brain decodes odours. It works like a puzzle, they say. Every odour molecule—*the key* — has a particular shape that fits a specific receptor cell—*the lock*. The brain then tells us we're smelling coffee, apple pie or roses. Nevertheless, some researchers, including Italian biophysicist Luca Turin, have reservations about this theory. It's all very well to have a lock and key, Turin says, but what *turns* the key? His hypothesis—once contentious but now gaining considerable support—asserts that smell is about vibrating molecules. He suggests the collaboration of shape *and* vibration may be the secret combination that turns the key.

Compelling research in the field of quantum biology offers further credibility to Turin's theory of vibration. A BBC documentary video demonstrates how the bonds that hold atoms together are like vibrating strings. Since different smells vibrate at different frequencies, smelling is rather like hearing, and smell molecules are playing music for our noses.

Meanwhile, the jury remains out as to the definitive answer to the mystery of how smell really works.

The Smell of Health

The current reality in North America's healthcare system often finds us sitting in waiting rooms for long periods prior to hurried ten-minute appointments with our physicians. This is a huge departure from the era when doctors spent a considerable amount of time with their patients and relied upon listening, palpating, observing and smelling to provide critical clues for diagnosis. The Greek physician Hippocrates—considered the father of western medicine—routinely examined his patient's breath, sweat, blood, urine, pus, earwax, phlegm and stool. And for some doctors, tasting their patient's urine was a necessary step for confirming diabetes. Not only was it recognized that disease could change the odour of bodily excretions, but the following observations were once general knowledge among physicians:

✧ The breath emits a sweet smell in the early stages of plague.

✧ Diabetes produces a fruity odour.

✧ Typhoid fever smells like baked bread.

✧ Smallpox smells sweet and pungent.

✧ Liver disease can smell fishy.

✧ Diphtheria smells mousy.

✧ Rheumatism is acidy.

✧ Kidney conditions are accompanied by a urinous odour.

After twenty years of nursing experience in hospitals, I can attest to the unpleasant smells that accompany illness, and I know that physicians would need to be suffering from a smell dysfunction not to be aware of the plethora of odours that are emitted from their patients. Regardless, doctors who personally assess olfactory clues have become a rare breed. Only once did I observe a surgeon who routinely sniffed the dressings of his post-surgical patients to rule out early signs of infection. However, I've recently been delighted to learn of several kindred spirits who continue to heed olfactory signals. One is American physician Dr. Andrew Bomback. In an article published in the *New England Journal of Medicine*, he laments not only the demise of the thorough physical exam but asserts that all he can learn from using his eyes, ears, hands and nose far outweigh the results of a litany of blood tests reviewed on a computer screen. He contends that smell's implications are as important as blood count levels or chest x-rays. Dr. Bomback also acknowledges that his own sense of smell has improved since the day he donned his long, white coat.[2]

Researchers determined decades ago that skin cancers emit specific odours that differ from normal skin. Though they were successful in deciphering each cancer's odour profile, they were uncertain how to accurately assess those odours in patients. This is apparently still a problem, yet I found it gratifying to learn that some physicians remain willing to exercise their olfactory dexterity when examining patients. A colleague informed me that an MD specializing in dermatology to whom she had been referred had leaned right in and *sniffed* the suspicious marks and moles on her neck and chest and then proceeded to cauterize one of them.

Move Over Bloodhounds

More recently, dogs have been trained for the task of detecting skin cancers, but it turns out the heightened smell acuity of dogs may be overrated, for who would have suspected we homo sapiens possess the same ability as bloodhounds for following a scent trail? A research team at the University of California, Berkeley demonstrated that we're not only capable of tracking scent, but we improve with practise. Volunteers, blindfolded, ears plugged and suited up in protective clothing, got down on their hands and knees, and with noses to the ground like sniffer dogs, they followed a chocolate scent trail over a grassy field. Two-thirds of the volunteers were able to follow the scent.[3] The research paper didn't report if a well-deserved treat—chocolate perhaps—awaited the human bloodhounds at the end of the trail.

At some point in humanity's uncertain future, we may have good cause to bring the innate diagnostic talents of our noses back into service. Research is validating that—through the sense of smell—some people can detect or be trained to detect when another person's immune system is on alert because bacteria has invaded their body. Within hours, laboratory volunteers were able to detect odour cues that signalled something smelled *off* in research participants whose immune systems had been artificially stimulated to appear under attack.

As further testament to our human olfactory sensitivity, Joy Milne, a former nurse in the UK, can detect Parkinson's disease in others. She became aware of this ability when, six years prior to her husband's diagnosis of Parkinson's, she had observed that he had begun to emit a musky, woody smell. She later came to realize she could detect this same odour in others with the condition. In a research project that included twelve participants, she was one hundred percent accurate in sniffing and identifying the T-shirts worn by the seven participants in the project who had Parkinson's.[4] It is now believed the disease triggers the release of an odorous chemical through the skin, and it's likely, the discovery will lead to the development of an early diagnostic test.

Technology Usurps Nature

For the present, our bodily specimens are dutifully deposited at a lab and rarely do they, or we, come under the examining nostrils of a physician. However, it's possible the collection of blood, urine and feces specimens will one day become obsolete. Quantum technologies are nosing their way into the health field as diagnostic tools and exhaling our breath-prints may soon be a routine part of medical checkups—much like being pulled over and given a breathalyzer test at the side of the road. Sophisticated breathalyzers, developed in the late 1980s and known as electronic noses or e-noses, are already diagnosing diseases like Multiple Sclerosis, Alzheimer's, Parkinson's and lung cancer. They're also sniffing out hormone levels as well as fertility and neurological conditions such as autism. And at some time in the future, when we're ill and under the blankets in the comfort of our homes, we may find ourselves blowing into our phones to be diagnosed on the other end of the line.

With the rampant rise of chronic disease in North America, the wish for physical and emotional health is predicted to be the biggest demand of the future. E-noses could be of enormous benefit, saving millions of dollars on invasive tests and waiting periods. Nevertheless, it is likely we'll be extending a further farewell to any expectation of the same level of personalized care we once had from our physicians.

Smell Deprivation

The absence of smell is described as being equivalent to participating in life in monochrome. I whine like a spoiled child when suffering from a head cold or stuffy nose that interferes with my olfactory functioning, particularly when it also deprives me of my sense of taste. I fully sympathize with freelance journalist Julie Bindel who lost her sense of smell for two weeks during a sinus infection. In finding it difficult not to panic, she writes, "The dread I had during those smell-free weeks was that if I never smelled again, how would I ever recall key moments in my life? How would I remember Charlie perfume along with my teenage years?" Mercifully, Julie woke one morning to the smell of coffee beans being ground by guests in her kitchen. Running around the house like a madwoman, she sniffed flowers, clothes, cough medicine, even her Deep Heat back pain cream, exclaiming that everything smelled glorious.[5]

Smell's Thieves

Sinus problems, colds, flu, nasal polyps, allergies, respiratory infections and runny noses make up eighty percent of all smell disorders. The majority of these conditions are temporary, but recovery can be slow. And in severe or chronic cases, the sense of smell doesn't always return to its original state. Other factors contributing to smell dysfunction are:

✧ exposure to toxic substances in the workplace or environment

✧ alcohol and drug abuse, cancer therapy, radiation

✧ diseases such as Alzheimer's, other forms of dementia and Parkinson's

✧ medications such as antibiotics, antidepressants, cholesterol or blood pressure-lowering drugs, and erectile dysfunction drugs

Smell can be lost suddenly through accidents or surgery. In fact, head trauma—which occurs most commonly in the under fifty years age group—is the second leading cause of smell impairment. Not much impact is necessary to result in brain damage, and once olfactory nerves are severed, they rarely reconnect, which precipitates a grave misfortune for victims who will spend the rest of their lives bereft of the pleasures of smell. As even heading a soccer ball can cause concussion-like symptoms, including smell loss, coaches are now discouraging the practice among young people whose brains are still developing. I grimace, too, when my granddaughter lands hard after a rugby tackle, but fortunately, as rugby gains popularity in North America, parents are imploring coaches and sports authorities to initiate the use of helmets.

Active babies can easily fall from changing tables or wiggle their way out of a parent's arms, land on a hard surface and suffer head trauma. When examined, the child may appear unharmed. As a result, such accidents are rarely later followed up for any sign of smell loss, which may have resulted from the fall. Unlike vision and hearing, smell tests are not included in routine health examinations. And since children don't miss something they've never known, the absence of the sense of smell can go undetected until much later in childhood and even into the teen years. Often parents don't realize there is an issue until, perhaps, they reprimand the child for something as simple as letting the toast burn. "Couldn't you smell it burning?" they ask and receive a bewildered "No" in reply. The lightbulb flicks on and the parents realize their child has never reacted to the reek of skunk, freshly spread manure on the garden or even the enticing aromas of food cooking on the stove. At this point, a physician may be consulted. Or the child grows up, making their way through life smell-less until they work out the loss on their own.

A family member introduced me to Miriam, a young woman who had begun to question whether her sense of smell and taste were as acute as those of other people. In her late teens, she realized she didn't react or object to smells as readily or as vehemently as her family members and friends reacted. When I questioned her further, she appeared to have a lower-than-normal acuity of both smell and taste, and I referred her to several established websites and books on smell disorders which I believed she'd find helpful. A few months after our initial contact, I received an email message from Miriam informing me she had recently learned from her parents that she had fallen on her head as a baby. It's unlikely she'll ever have conclusive evidence as to whether that fall caused permanent impairment to her olfactory functioning. However, what moved me about Miriam's story is that she loves to cook. And because she believed she could turn her talent into a career despite her sensory limitations, she entered chef school following high school graduation. I say bravo! And I look forward to following her progress.

The Forgotten Sense

Being born without a sense of smell—congenital anosmia—can occur, though it is a rare condition, and the cause is unknown. Just under five percent of the population suffer from permanent *anosmia,* the complete inability to detect odours. But a startling number of people in the western world have some form of diminished ability to smell or discriminate between odours, and the incidence appears to be rising. People confide in me woeful tales of friends or family members who cope with a smell dysfunction. Most sufferers assume nothing can be done for them and they simply need to live with it. Such an attitude isn't surprising. Throughout much of the twentieth century, olfaction received little attention within the medical community in comparison with vision and hearing, and physicians today still find themselves at a loss when dealing with patients with smell disorders. Fortunately, the tide is turning, and the sense of smell is beginning to garner the attention it deserves.

Losing Life's Savour

Mealtimes were always my father's favourite time of day, particularly as he aged and his hearing and eyesight dimmed, and therefore it was unexpected when he sternly announced one day in his ninety-eighth year that the nursing home was adding cardboard to his meals. Since Dad resided in a respectable establishment, we assured him it was unlikely this was the case, suggesting that perhaps his sense of smell was decreasing and affecting his taste buds. He refused to accept our reasoning and persisted in his cardboard additive theory until his death at the age of 102.

Though my father retained his olfactory functions well into old age, unsettling research published in 2014 has revealed that smell loss can be an early symptom of the onset of neurodegenerative diseases such as Alzheimer's and Parkinson's. According to Dr. Jayant M. Pinto of the University of Chicago, when people become incapable of recognizing *common* smells in their later years, there is a greater likelihood they could die within five years than there is if they are coping with a terminal illness. He explains that the smell loss isn't a *cause* of death but rather a warning signal that neurological damage is present. In the study—which included over 3,000 people between the ages of fifty-seven and eighty-five—close to forty percent of those who lost the ability to recognize common smells died within five years. This was in comparison with ten percent of those in the study with a normal sense of smell.[6]

With aging, there is normally some deterioration in all our senses, and smell is no exception, being most acute in childhood and gradually declining over a lifetime. But my attitude is to use it or lose it. Those who cultivate an appreciation for this magnificent sense often continue to enjoy its delights into old age. In fact, being mindful and attentive to all of our senses throughout our lifetimes heightens and preserves them in our consciousness. If one sense deteriorates significantly or is lost, we can continue to engage with it from memory. Beethoven is an example. After he had become totally deaf, he went on to compose his majestic Ninth Symphony because music had remained alive in his memory. The renowned twentieth-century perfumer Jean Carles created his most famous perfumes in his later years—Ma Griffe, Miss Dior, Tabu—after he had suffered the complete loss of smell. His olfactory memory had remained alive. And I learned of a woman who was deprived of her sense of smell after being kicked in the head by a horse. The loss was particularly devastating because she loved to cook, but the tragedy didn't prevent her from continuing to labour with love in her kitchen. When she needed assistance, her family, friends and neighbours happily volunteered to be her taste testers.

Pleasures of the Palate

To ensure the survival of our species, we were endowed with five basic taste cravings: sweet, sour, bitter, salty and umami (savoury). Some nutrition experts suggest pungent and astringent belong on the list as well. By satisfying our cravings for these foods, we provide the body with nutrients that are critical to its healthy functioning. However, our enjoyment of food would be significantly lessened if we were limited to these cravings, and this is where the gift of flavour comes into the culinary picture. Anything over and above the basic taste cravings is flavour, which is produced by smell. Aside from the abundance of taste buds prevalent in our oral cavities, receptor cells for taste are also located high up in our nasal passages so that eighty to ninety percent of what we perceive as taste is owed to smell.

Most people derive great pleasure from eating, yet when asked the tough question—which of your five senses would you be willing to relinquish—over fifty percent choose smell followed by taste, touch, hearing and sight, in that order. A sobering survey taken in 2011 found that if forced to make a choice, fifty percent of those between the ages of 16 and 30 would give up smell before giving up their smartphones or laptops. However, those who would choose to give up smell have either forgotten or are unaware that their decision would also mean forgoing their sense of taste. In my class, "Thriving with Your Sense of Smell," I witness people's reactions when they experience proof of this fundamental connection between smell and taste. I have them chew jellybeans and allow them to savour the flavour for several minutes before asking them to pinch their nostrils closed. Many are astonished. Though they continue to sense a vague sweetness, the flavours of the jellybeans, whether red, green, yellow or black, are no longer discernible.

Smell and taste work in concert. As the eighteenth-century French gastronome Brillat-Savarin aptly described this combination of senses, "They are but a single composite sense whose laboratory is the mouth and its chimney the nose."[7]   Nowhere is there a better example of the focused attention given to the fusion of taste and smell than in wine tasting. That popular ritual of taking a swig of wine, holding it in the mouth and swilling it like mouthwash prior to spitting it out is all about oxygenating the wine to get the flavour into the nose...to catch the bouquet... to taste the fragrance. Those with careers in the olfactory arts tend to participate with gusto in both wine tasting and cooking since a foundation in these disciplines teaches discernment of the subtle distinctions in odour and taste. Each of these vocations uses similar descriptive language such as zesty, flat, rich, spicy, dry, sweet, crisp, notes, bouquets and blends.

Beyond the Nose

Until very recently, it was believed that smell receptors are present exclusively within the nasal cavity. Now groundbreaking evidence is establishing it's not only our noses that are doing the smelling, but our entire bodies are sniffing and engaged in supporting the functioning of our physiology. According to the July 2018 issue of the medical publication *Physiological Reviews,* in over 200 studies, smell and taste receptors have been discovered in the most unlikely places, including the lungs, kidneys, sperm, muscles, tissues and skin. Scientists are calling them "extra-nasal" receptors and they appear to act as chemical sensors that perform a wide variety of functions, such as regulating blood pressure, reducing the spread of liver and colon cancer cells, speeding up wound healing and aiding digestion.[8]

As ongoing research continues to unravel the complexity and mystery that encompass the sense of smell, it's apparent we can no longer take for granted this tool of immeasurable value which penetrates, influences, guides and protects many diverse aspects of our lives.

Vetiver
Vetiveria zizanioides

Botanical Family:	*Gramineae*
Country of Origin:	Indonesia, India, Haiti, Réunion, Brazil
Fragrance Group:	Base note
Aroma:	Earthy, musty with rich woody undertones
Extraction Process:	Steam distillation
Derived From:	Perennial grass and dried, ground roots
Valuable Uses:	Physical: antiseptic, rheumatic conditions, circulatory tonic, anti-parasitic
	Emotional/Mental/Spiritual: reduces nervous tension, calming, grounding
Of Added Interest:	When woven with floor matting and window coverings, the grass imparts fragrance and deters insects.
Contraindications:	None known

Initiation into Smell School

$\mathcal{F}$ollowing my life-changing inhalation of lavender essential oil, I yearned for a deeper understanding of the essential character of the numinous essences newly arrived and neatly arranged on the shelves of my local health food store. Their beauty seduced my sensory imagination, yet I questioned what had impelled the alchemists in centuries past to toil so tediously to extract what they believed to be the liquid gold of plants. For many, it is enough to hold a flower in the hand to sniff ... and perhaps sigh ... while marveling at its intricacy and perfection. The nineteenth-century English perfumer Septimus Piesse expressed his understanding of the striving of the alchemists when he wrote, "The exquisite pleasure derived from smelling fragrant flowers would almost instinctively induce man to attempt to separate the odiferous principle from them."[9]

Alchemy, shrouded in mystery and secrecy, was practiced throughout the ages in Europe and Asia. Believed to have its origins in pre-pharaonic Egypt, its earliest writings date back to the third and fourth centuries in Alexandria, Egypt. The word "chemistry," derived from the word alchemy and "chemical" from the ancient Greek root *chemia*, means "transmutation"—changing one thing to another, such as a base metal to gold or a sick body to a healthy one. Early physicians extracted the juices from plants for medicinal purposes, causing some historians to believe that alchemy simply meant the expression of plant juice. The alchemists themselves referred to the liquids they distilled as the quinta essentia or quintessence of the substance, and in ancient and medieval philosophy, quintessence was considered the highest element permeating all nature. Drawn from raw materials and converted to its purest and most concentrated form, it was considered the essence of a thing—its life force, soul, spirit, nature, heart, crux. In his cult novel *Perfume,* author Patrick Süskind compares the process to snatching a plant's scented soul.

In pursuit of further knowledge of olfaction and its relationship to aromatic plants, I chanced upon a small ad in a local newspaper promoting an aromatherapy course that was coming to Vancouver. The company, Aromatherapy Seminars, was offering a two-part program that began with a mandatory home-study component. It was 1994. The timing was right in the scheme of my life and I immediately enrolled. Upon the arrival of the study materials, I was like a giddy child on Christmas morning, reaching into her stocking to snatch up one delight after another. However, this time my pleasure came from digging deep to retrieve a small but bulging package that held twenty-three jewel-coloured sample vials of a selection of essential oils—ylang ylang, cypress, rosewood, geranium, jasmine and chamomile, to name a few. Sniffing the contents of that simple, unadorned package immersed me in a universe of odours I'd never before experienced, and it held more attraction for my olfactory sensibility than all the pricey perfumes of Paris. (Years later and long after the liquids in the vials had evaporated, their residual aromas lingered on, and one whiff inside that little bag would instantly transport me back in time to my virginal venture into aromatherapy.)

I delved hungrily into the Aromatherapy Seminars home study workbook and began an exploration of a long list of topics: the physiology and psychology of smell, plant evolution, the history of aromatics, essential oil monographs, essential oil blending and a therapeutic index of ailments.

Back to the Future

Plant-based aromatics, I learned, have been integrated into the daily lives of peoples of all cultures throughout recorded history. Esteemed as aphrodisiacs, as remedies in the prevention and treatment of illness and as sweet-scented balms for the soul, they trail a legacy of mystery, magic and healing lore. It may have been fire that initiated humankind's enduring connection with fragrance. The word perfume is derived from the Latin *par fumum*—through smoke. I envision our early ancestors roaming the land and settling around campfires at night, tossing leaves, twigs and branches into the fire and turning their noses in curiosity toward the new and enticing aromas that arose from the flames. As time progressed and their consciousness expanded, they explored, experimented and came to know the many benefits offered by the plant kingdom. Subsequently, they created rituals in their efforts to control storms, floods and other unpredictable weather patterns. Smoke from woods, gums and resins burning on altars spiraled heavenward as offerings to appease and please the "sky father." Today we see indications of the legacies of aromatic plants from ancient civilizations and advanced societies displayed in the treasures uncovered in archaeological excavations, in hieroglyphics in caves, in inscriptions on papyri and tombs and in the pages of classical literature.

A four-day live seminar followed the completion of the Aromatherapy Seminars home-study assignments, a case study and an honour test, and when I entered the subtly fragranced classroom of a downtown Vancouver hotel that first morning of the seminar, the room was buzzing with the anticipation of the thirty or so participants. The seminar leaders were two of a growing number of educators responsible for introducing aromatherapy to North America. Marcel Lavabre, born and raised in the lavender-growing region of southern France, had studied aromatherapy since 1974 and had worked in France supervising all areas of essential oil production. Michael Scholes, from England, had previously been immersed in researching alternative health therapies in the UK, yet he had always searched for what he called "the missing piece." One day in the late 1980s, while wandering the aisles of a health fair in

London, he had come upon a table displaying small glass bottles. One of the two Frenchmen who stood behind the table was Daniel Pénoël, a medical doctor and one of the leading proponents of aroma medicine in France. The other, Pierre Franchomme, a bio-chemist, had been researching the properties of essential oils since 1959. The two were renowned in their own country for their collaborative work and for their textbook *L'aromathérapie exactement (Exact Aromatherapy)*.

Scholes' quest for the "missing piece" was fulfilled that day. He learned from the two Frenchmen that aromatherapy had been popular in France for more than a decade, and by participating in the health fair, they were hoping to meet and train others who would take aromatherapy education into North America's enormous untapped market. Following a period of intense study with Dr. Pénoël, Scholes emigrated to the US, founded Aromatherapy Seminars and promoted his newly found passion and programs across the continent. The late Rae Dunphy and her husband Jeff Dunphy of True Essence Aromatherapy (now Rae Dunphy Aromatics), supplied the essential oils and related materials for the course. They were early pioneers of aromatherapy in Canada and a respected influence in aromatherapy education.

Swathed in Aroma

Our instructors had a rapt and receptive audience, each of us aware we were on the cutting edge of a new and powerful healing modality—the therapeutic use of plant-derived aromatic essences for promoting physical and psychological well-being. And it was the only health modality based on the sense of smell. Scent strips saturated with bergamot, basil, chamomile and a multitude of other essential oils were distributed one at a time. Sitting quietly, eyes closed to lessen distraction, we held each scent strip at chest level and rotated it in a circular motion to create a vortex for the rising aroma. Slowly raising the strip under our nostrils, we inhaled deeply while attempting to sense where the aroma travelled in our bodies—smelling, feeling, tasting, listening and allowing it to reveal its character, shape, colour and nuance.

On learning that the highly concentrated and volatile energy stored in a plant's ducts and glandular hairs is responsible for its aroma, I began to comprehend the tireless zeal of the alchemists in previous centuries. They came to understand that nature's seductive scents are messengers of communication between species, sending and receiving signals that lure beneficial insects and act as hormones for protecting plants from stress, disease and drought. They discovered that a reciprocal relationship exists between plants and humans as well and that aromatic plant oils function as therapeutic agents in our human domain. Today distillers in fields and factories worldwide, particularly in developing countries, extract these powerful plant energies along with their aromas by submerging plant material—petals, herbs, leaves, seeds, roots and woods—into large vats of water. The brew is gently simmered until steam builds up, the ducts soften, and the oils are released. The resultant odiferous drops, the essential oils, are siphoned into a waiting receptacle. Fragrant floral waters and hydrolats such as rose, orange blossom, chamomile and geranium are by-products of the distillation process and remain in the still. Many of them contain water-soluble active ingredients, which are gentle and therapeutic in their own right and are highly beneficial in skin care, wound healing and emotional healing.

Other methods for extracting essential oils include *carbon dioxide extraction and cold expression.* The latter is a process of pressing the fragrant and zesty essential oils from the rinds of citrus plants—lemons, limes, oranges, grapefruit and the bergamot orange. The chemical structure of each essential oil is highly complex and dependent upon:

✧ the part of the plant distilled (roots, leaves, bark, flower petals)

✧ the method of extraction

✧ the time of day of extraction

The active molecules present in each essential oil determine its therapeutic effects on our physiology and psychology. For instance:

✧ Clove and cinnamon—strong smelling and fiery in nature—are stimulants with highly effective antiseptics properties. They can also be skin irritants.

✧ Rosemary, peppermint and geranium are energizing and have antibacterial, antiviral and germicidal properties.

✧ Jasmine can induce euphoria and dispel the concerns of the moment.

✧ Roman chamomile, lavender and mandarin act on the central nervous system to soothe tension and anxiety and are gentle enough to lull a baby into slumber.

Modes of Application

The methods for employing essential oils are diverse and are based on the desired outcome. They may be directed into the respiratory system through inhalation from the bottle or a tissue, steam inhalation, a diffuser or room spray. Alternately, when used in a bath, foot bath, massage, compress, body wrap or facial, the molecules are absorbed into the skin. Examples of application include:

✧ Tenting the head with a towel and inhaling the steam from a bowl of hot water infused with several drops of eucalyptus for easing bronchial congestion while combating infection.

✧ Stroking a diluted blend of peppermint, basil and lavender on the forehead, temples and back of the neck to soothe a headache.

✧ Massaging chamomile, lavender, marjoram and clary sage onto the arms, shoulders and back to dispel muscle aches and to release nervous tension.

** Numerous books on aromatherapy that offer in-depth guidance on the benefits and application of essential oils are available in bookstores.

A Word of Caution

Essential oils are powerful, concentrated substances and each drop is considered equivalent to one ounce of plant material. Responsibility in their use is essential, particularly in pregnancy, while breastfeeding, with infants, small children, pets, the elderly and those with skin sensitivities, allergies, asthma and multiple chemical sensitivities. Other points to consider are:

✧ Essential oils need to be diluted in a carrier oil (e.g., almond, coconut or jojoba) for application on the skin. A patch test before use is recommended for those with sensitive skin.

✧ Discretion is required when diffusing essential oils.

✧ Oral ingestion is strongly discouraged unless one is under the guidance of a knowledgeable practitioner.

✧ To avoid the low-grade, adulterated and ineffectual oils and products that have flooded the market, the purchase of high-quality essential oils from a respected source is highly recommended.

✧ Ideally, the label on an essential oil bottle will display the following information:

  • Common name of the plant (e.g., rosemary)

  • Latin name (e.g., *rosmarinus officinalis*)

  • Part of the plant distilled (e.g., flowers, leaves, bark, roots)

  • Country of origin

  • Extraction method (e.g., steam-distilled or cold expression)

  • Product warnings (e.g., Keep out of reach of children. Keep away from eyes. Avoid in pregnancy. Not for internal use.)

Too Late to Turn Back

Never have I have been so enthusiastic about entering a classroom than during my initiation into smell school. My knowledge, understanding and respect for the sense of smell and the odours and aromas of the natural world, were enhanced a thousand-fold, and though the seminar instructors had cautioned us that entering the field of aromatherapy could expose us to a delightful form of addiction, for me the warning came too late. Lavender had captured my olfactory attention, but once I'd plunged my nose into that little bag of oils that had arrived in my mailbox, I had become wholeheartedly hooked. Following the two-part Aromatherapy Seminars program, many of us continued our studies and became practitioners, teachers, essential oil distributors and retail merchants. From this latter group, highly successful businesses emerged including Aroma Joy (now Saje Natural Wellness) which currently boasts stores across Canada and has recently entered the US market, and Escents Aromatherapy, which has become an international brand. Both businesses were launched on Vancouver's North Shore in the early 1990s. Rae Dunphy Aromatics in Calgary, in business since 1988, remains a leader in the field of aromatherapy in Canada.

Scent Trails Proliferate

Rumours of the healing benefits of olfaction enhanced by the beauty of nature's essential oils descended upon North America like fragrant fireworks. Educational opportunities in aromatherapy proliferated and newly trained teachers, instructors and essential oil suppliers—many being novices in the field themselves—were as enthusiastic and dedicated as their students. A particularly memorable occasion for me in those early days was crossing the Canada/US border in 1994 with a carload of eager colleagues and driving 700 miles to attend a rousing Young Living Essential Oils convention in Coeur d'Alene, Idaho. Young Living's founder and energetic entrepreneur, the late Gary Young (1949-2018), knew a good thing when he saw it—or rather, when he smelled it—the potential for marketing essential oils in a multi-level business format. As an early student of Aromatherapy Seminars, Young had also become wholeheartedly hooked. He continued to educate himself in the new therapy and swiftly progressed in bringing aromatherapy to the aroma-loving, wellness-seeking masses. Following the upbeat convention in Idaho for motivating hundreds of Young

Living distributors, my colleagues and I got down on our knees planting lavender seedlings in the fields of Young's farm, recently purchased for harvesting and distilling oils for his burgeoning new company.

Once back in Canada, highly motivated and on a mission to further my education in olfaction in conjunction with plant aromatics, I enrolled in an intensive program that included aromatherapy massage. Based on the philosophy and style of aromatherapy practiced in England at the time, it promoted a holistic approach to healing as opposed to the modern-day method of treating symptoms that manifest solely on the physical level. Each of us express symptoms on multiple levels—physical, emotional, mental and spiritual—and ideally all are taken into consideration in order for one to be treated as a dynamic whole. I learned how to conduct an in-depth consultation and prepare a customized blend of essential oils that would suit each client's individual needs. And I was trained in light lymphatic aromatherapy massage—a restorative and balancing technique that gently stimulates the lymphatic system and clears it of waste. Through massage, the healing benefits of essential oils are transported into the bloodstream, and their aromas serve to enhance the treatment.

Launching a New Career

One year later and in possession of a certificate identifying me as a Certified Aromatherapist along with a previous certification in Reflexology, I set up a studio, hung out my shingle, and became a member of the newly organized provincial association, the British Columbia Association of Practicing Aromatherapists (BCAPA). However, I learned early in the debut of my new career that despite my knowledge, training and enthusiasm in this new therapy of healing with smell, promoting my skills to a skeptical public wasn't going to be an easy sell. Friends, family and strangers alike looked at me askance, even with bemusement, when I proudly proclaimed my recent hard-earned designation as an aromatherapist. "You're a what?" they'd ask.

Nevertheless, I was determined not to become discouraged or deterred in my purpose—after all, France's Dr. Daniel Pénoël considered aromatic matter, "the immune system of humanity."[10] In promoting my cause as well as my practice, I regaled the benefits of aromatherapy to students at the local alternative high school, to teachers on their professional development days and in continuing education classes, spas, retreat centres and health fairs. I wrote articles for aromatherapy publications and was interviewed on several occasions by a local newspaper. Though I networked with members of my professional association, a special connection helped to sustain me during those early years when I felt isolated in my cause. I developed a friendship with Leah Morgan, an energetic, passionate and determined young aromatherapist who had recently started up a wholesale business called Healingscents Aromatherapy. Our relationship kept me inspired and motivated and continues to do so to this day.

Through word of mouth, my practice—Scent and Soul Aromatherapy—slowly grew. My typical clients tended to be stressed, overworked and under-nurtured women, and my objective was to offer them solace, relaxation and restoration. Aromatherapy assists in overcoming the separation that exists in our modern world between body, mind, emotions and spirit. Soothing, nurturing touch accompanied with a customized blend of essential oils supports that process. One of my clients, a powerhouse in her work and in her community, confessed at the conclusion of a massage that it had been many years since she had been able to drop into such a deep state of relaxation. She was uncertain how to integrate this feeling within herself in order to return to the tasks remaining in her day. I explained it was of vital importance for her peace of mind and well-being to remain in that state for a period of time before resuming her daily routine. She later told me that rather than detouring to the grocery store following her massage, she had returned home, rested quietly with a cup of tea for an hour and cancelled her evening engagement. In making these simple changes, she had given herself the quiet time she desperately craved, required and deserved. And she'd had the best sleep she'd had in months.

Since reflexes on the feet can indicate to a practitioner what is out of tune in a client's body, and massage and manipulation of these reflexes can be profoundly relaxing, I integrated Aroma Reflexology treatments into my services. Each sixty-minute session ended with a soothing foot and lower leg massage customized with essential oils. This treatment was particularly popular with men. Though the majority of these fellows promptly fell asleep in my reclining chair and snored throughout the session, they departed, appearing relaxed and revitalized as though a great weight had been lifted from their shoulders.

While establishing my new career in Canada, I found it frustrating that other parts of the world were far ahead of us. For example, medical doctors in France were writing prescriptions for essential oil preparations and nurses in England were already introducing aromatherapy into hospital settings. Yet the concept that aromas had the potential to enhance health remained a curiosity here in North America. Unpleasant odours, like the wretched smells of cough, stomach and constipation remedies and the medicinal smells of hospital corridors, were associated with ill health. Pleasing aromas went hand in hand with perfume and pleasure but not with healing. My sole consolation was knowing that a period of time is usually necessary before a radical new concept, reaches its tipping point and becomes widely known and accepted.

It was another decade and well into the twenty-first century before aromatherapy's tipping point materialized in North America. In the meantime, a major force had intervened, hampering the recognition and growth of this beautiful healing modality as a bona fide therapy. That force was big business. Olfactory research on the psychology of smell was burgeoning in research labs throughout North America and Europe—funded principally by the fragrance industry—and it wasn't long before large corporations got a whiff of the results of the research. Certain scents, they were learning, not only influence the psyche but can make consumers spend more freely. Propelled into action by the smell of money, they churned out so-called aromatherapy products: dish and laundry detergents, bath and body care products, candles and all manner of scented trivia. And to further defeat aromatherapy's cause, the majority of these products were fragranced with artificial scents, not therapeutic essential oils.

Aromatherapy had been hijacked. It was history repeating itself.

Bergamot
Citrus bergamia

Botanical Family:	*Rutaceae*
Country of Origin:	Italy, Ivory Coast, Tunisia, Morocco
Fragrance Group:	Top note
Aroma:	Rich, sweet, lemony-orange, hint of floral
Extraction Process:	Cold expression
Derived From:	Rind of the fruit
Valuable Uses:	Physical: stimulant, digestive, antispasmodic, anti-infectious, useful for bladder infections
	Emotional/Mental/Spiritual: calming, relaxing, balancing, uplifting; relieves insomnia, encourages joy and harmony
Of Added Interest:	Bergamot is a popular flavouring in Earl Grey tea.
Contraindications:	Increases skin photosensitivity; when applied to the skin avoid sunlight on area of application for twelve hours.

Loss of Aromatics as Remedies

When applying a perfume or preparing an aromatic remedy, I often reflect that I am participating in a ritual that has been part of our human heritage for thousands of years. In the first century BC, Cleopatra perfumed her body in readiness for love and filled her boudoir with roses. And since ancient times the camphorous herb rosemary—bracing and purifying—has fortified the brain and cleared congestion. However, between the eighteenth and twentieth centuries, the western world turned away almost overnight from the preparations and perfumes that had sustained it for more than fifty centuries. Through my research I've uncovered a series of turning points within that period that destroyed humankind's respect for the relationship between the sense of smell and nature's aromatics.

The arrival of the Renaissance in the fourteenth century had brought a flowering of literature, language, arts and medicine into Europe, and newly opened trade routes to the east provided an influx of unfamiliar plants, spices and exotic flowers. The mild, sunny climate of southern France proved ideally suited to the production of these aromatic plants, and by the seventeenth century its rolling hills were resplendent with hues of fuchsia, violet and gold, and scents of orange blossom. lavender, jasmine and rose mingling with heady herbs and zesty citruses perfumed the air. Fragrant plants not only provided raw material for the blossoming perfume industry but were used as preventatives against illness. It was commonplace for twigs, leaves, flowers and herbs to be strewn on floors and burned in hearths to ward off the plague. In fact, in a village in France called Sauve it was observed that people who worked with fragrant botanicals were less likely to succumb to illness.

For the next three centuries French perfumers and pharmacists worked side by side in their apothecaries preparing remedies from the bounty of botanicals in the fields. They provided small bouquets of flowers and herbs called tussie-mussies to be sniffed for protection against disease, and they offered mood-elevating sachets as relief from melancholy. Those who could afford it splashed their faces and bodies with fragrant waters—also called toilet waters—prepared from herbs, essential oils and floral waters steeped in spirits. These concoctions, popular across Europe for their hygienic and health-enhancing properties, were also consumed internally as tonics. One such European preparation called Aqua Mirabilis, prepared from cardamom, cloves, ginger, mace and nutmeg and consumed for digestive ailments, was hailed as a miracle cure.

I imagine I would have felt right in my element working in a French apothecary in the seventeenth century, compounding, infusing and melding all manner of therapeutic concoctions like tussie-mussies, toilet waters, balms and salves, though women in that era weren't officially recognized as professionals by the guilds. My career may have taken a decidedly different turn had I known that at one time pharmacists and perfumers had worked together formulating prescriptions and blending perfumes. (I do regret that the subject of odiferous plants as medicines wasn't included in my nursing curriculum or even referenced in my textbooks. I had found pharmacology somewhat dry and unengaging, but researching aromatics as medicines might have lit a fire under me.)

By the eighteenth century, France was producing exceptionally high yields of fragrant crops, and the southern town of Grasse had established itself as the largest centre of aromatic culture in the world. Then, as methods for extracting aromas from these plants became more sophisticated and efficient, and France's perfumers enjoyed a more diverse palette of essences to work with, the demand for their creations soared throughout the country and even beyond its borders. However, while the relationship between perfumers and pharmacists had been respectful and harmonious until this time, grumblings began to surface. The issue was labeling. Most products prepared in apothecary shops required the labelling of ingredients, but as a demand for the purely aesthetic value of perfume increased, perfumers began to resist divulging the secret ingredients of their formulae. To resolve the conflict, they lobbied the government, demanding that their fragrant compositions be allowed to remain unlabeled. Their request was granted in 1810, and this bold move resulted in separate statuses being decreed for perfumers and pharmacists.

Cloning Nature

In the mid-1800s the new science of synthetic chemistry began isolating and replicating the scents of nature. In 1868 when the soft, new-mown hay aroma of the tonka bean was synthesized from coal tar, it was renamed coumarin and became the first synthetic substance to be used in perfumery. When the aroma of the vanilla bean was synthesized, it became known as vanillin. Since perfumers of that era had enjoyed a long tradition of working with plant materials of natural origin, they were slow to warm to the radical new artificial offerings, but the tempting array of fragrance chemicals that promised endless innovation—and endless profit—proved irresistible. As synthetic aromas began to replace the aromatic bounty harvested from the fields, many of the traditional products became unacceptable for internal use, contributing to the demise of aromatic preparations as remedies. For example, it was necessary to relegate toilet waters for external usage only, and the therapeutic tussie-mussie transitioned to the purely aesthetic nosegay popular in the Victorian era. By the mid-nineteenth century, the perfume industry in France had changed dramatically, and there appeared to be no turning back to the old ways.

41

The Lure of the Artificial

✧ Synthetics are stable and guarantee odour consistency in perfumers' formulas. In comparison, the aromas extracted from plants can vary from season to season depending on weather and soil conditions.

✧ Synthetics are colourless. Like the enthusiastic acceptance of white bread when first introduced in the nineteenth century, synthetic aromas guaranteed that perfumes—by now coveted, costly and showcased in elegant glass bottles—were considered "modern" by no longer displaying their primitive colours and hues.

✧ Synthetic scents have staying power and linger longer on the skin.

✧ Synthetics offer perfumers an endless array of new scents to add to their palettes.

✧ Synthetic chemicals can be produced in large quantities and are a bargain in comparison to the high costs of plant production.

The Great Sanitary Reform

Another critical piece in this historical olfactory narrative is the fallout that resulted from the change in living standards in European cities in the seventeenth century. Rapid population growth caused deplorable sanitary conditions: chamber pots were dumped onto sidewalks, corpses rotted above ground in cemeteries, tanners skinned their hides within city limits and dead animals were tossed into ditches and rivers. Stench was unavoidable. Yet in his treatise, *The Foul and the Fragrant*, French historian Alain Corbin asserts that overall, an indifference to malodours existed in France up until the mid-eighteenth century. Both pleasant and putrid smells were accepted as part of the human condition. But a cultural shift was coming that would change this attitude. Influenced by advances in chemistry, pharmacists, chemists and physicians initiated a movement to address public health, issuing dire warnings to the populace about the connection between bad smells, disease and death. Their warnings precipitated hysteria among the masses, and smell became so emotionally charged that people became less and less tolerant of foul odours. In Corbin's words, "It was as if thresholds of tolerance had been abruptly lowered ... all the evidence suggests that scientific theory played a crucial role in this lowering of thresholds." [11]

Consequently, stringent measures for improving hygiene were implemented. Bad smells were to be avoided at all costs, and the chemists emphasized that *real* disinfectants had to destroy substances in order to be effective. Fumigation with new and powerful chemicals such as chlorine was introduced, and armed with their potent new chemicals, chemists began discrediting the value of natural aromatics. This resulted in a government decree called *Halle's Official Code* that denounced the antiseptic and therapeutic properties of naturally odorous materials and caused a complete break with traditional attitudes.

Improvements in sanitary structures such as sewer networks and waste management systems were a godsend benefiting mankind to this day. Yet, at the same time, the introduction of toxic chemicals into everyday use in tandem with the devaluation of natural antiseptics was one giant leap backward. I also bemoan the demotion of the sense of smell itself that befell the western world when the Enlightenment, which heralded the so-called Age of Reason, spread across Europe during the eighteenth century. People began to deviate from earlier eras when intuition had balanced intellect, an intelligent awareness of the properties of plants and their remedies had reigned, and aromatics were used to treat all manner of afflictions. As physicians and modern pharmacists with their medicine-laden shelves replaced the apothecaries and began competing for patient fees, people began to relinquish responsibility for their health.

In the lead-up to the twentieth century, nature's fragrant therapeutics were discredited, and the sense of smell fell from grace within the hierarchy of the senses. This two-fold misfortune was responsible in part for the demise of fifty centuries of scent-centric humanity. The western world's departure from a reliance on the kindred connection between the sense of smell and well-being resulted in:

✧ a heightened fear of foul odours

✧ the introduction of strong chemicals as the solution for fighting foul odours and preventing disease

✧ the discredit and dismissal of natural aromatics as remedies and disinfectants

✧ the separation of perfumes from pharmaceuticals

✧ the introduction of synthetic chemicals into aromatic preparations, resulting in a separation from nature's pharmacy

✧ the separation of mind and body by scientists and philosophers

✧ the demotion of the sense of smell to the bottom of the hierarchy of the senses

Aromatics Prevail

In spite of the general drive away from natural products, a handful of European science and medical professionals remained steadfast on the trail of essential oil research. British surgeon Dr. Joseph Lister is one example. Famed for initiating the use of antiseptics in surgery, Lister had also isolated the anti-infectious components of essential oils. His formula for Listerine mouthwash, named after him in 1879, contained the essential oils of eucalyptus, thyme and peppermint. Throughout much of my father's adult life, a glass bottle of Listerine sat on his bathroom counter like a religious icon and was a regular player in his morning routine, and I sometimes wonder if his daily gargle contributed to his achieving centenarian status. Listerine lives on to this day, stacked high on pharmacy shelves and still displaying its bold black label. The small glass bottles that held the original, amber-tinged antiseptic formula of alcohol and essential oils that sat on our bathroom shelf were replaced in 1992 with gargantuan-sized plastic jugs of mouthwash in all the colours of the rainbow. However, the medicinal ingredients listed on the label—which promise to kill up to ninety-nine percent of the bacteria that cause gingivitis and bad breath—remain the same: essential oils of eucalyptus, thyme and peppermint. But Listerine's non-medicinal ingredients—which I jotted down from a bottle displayed in a local pharmacy—now include: water in a wide assortment of colours (for example green 3), aroma for flavour, benzoic acid, methyl salicylate, polymer 407, propylene glycol, sodium benzoate, sodium lauryl sulfate, sodium saccharine, sorbitol, sucrose and yellow 10.

Lister's groundbreaking work encouraged a resurgence of interest in essential oils within scientific circles, and as a result, research papers expounding the anti-infectious virtues of essential oils were widely published in Europe. But in 1928, Alexander Fleming isolated penicillin, laying the foundation for germ theory and antibiotics. And since essential oils—many of them powerful anti-infectious medicines in their own right—were derived from nature, it was illegal to patent them, and it remains that way today. As such, regardless of the abundant documentation on the pharmacology of essential oils available in French and German literature, there has never been any financial advantage for the pharmaceutical industry or private corporations to fund essential oil research.

We Had It, We Lost It, We Got It Back

If I have a hero in the realm of aroma medicine, it's René-Maurice Gattefossé (1881–1950) who was responsible for resurrecting the medicinal use of aromatics from history's fragrant ashes. He worked as a perfume chemist in Gattefossé Establishments, a family business that produced and provided essential oils, chemicals and other raw materials for the perfume trade. Throughout my studies, I rarely came across an aromatherapy textbook that didn't reference the near tragedy that altered the life of this early proponent of aromatherapy. In recounting that fateful day, he wrote:

"... after a laboratory explosion covered me with burning substances which I extinguished by rolling on a grassy lawn, both my hands were covered with a rapidly developing gas gangrene. Just one rinse with lavender essence [essential oil] stopped the 'gasification of the tissue.' This

45

treatment was followed by profuse sweating and healing began the next day."[12]

Gas gangrene is a medical emergency. The organism *clostridium perfringens* invades damaged skin, producing gas in the tissues. Infection spreads rapidly and, if not treated, can lead to death within twenty-four to forty-eight hours, yet Gattefossé claimed that one desperate rinse with lavender essential oil saved his life. He was unaware at the time of lavender's profound antiseptic and healing properties, but they kicked in immediately to stem the encroaching infection. Mercifully, its analgesic properties would have eased his agonizing pain, and to top off these near-miraculous effects, it's likely that lavender's sedative qualities benefited him throughout the traumatic event. Fortunately, Gattefossé not only made a full recovery, but his experience transformed his life along with the future of aroma medicine. It's no surprise he went on to devote himself to probing the therapeutic properties of essential oils. While experimenting with a selection of oils on the injuries of soldiers in WW1, he noted exceptional results in the area of wound healing—wounds free from the inflammation, itching and pain that often accompanied the antiseptics in common use at the time.

Gattefossé is the man who conceived the term aromatherapy a century ago, and today it is a household word. His seminal work, translated and published in 1937 as *Gattefossé's Aromatherapy*, influenced countless followers, including esteemed French medical and science professionals, Jean Valnet, Pierre Franchomme, Paul Belaiche and Daniel Pénoël. To this day, France is renowned for achieving the most advanced clinical research in aroma medicine, and as a result, Gattefossé came to be called "the father of aromatherapy."

Ode to Lavender

Lavender essential oil is one item I would choose to have with me for healing, comfort and hygienic purposes should I be stranded on a desert island. Otherwise, it's an essential commodity in my everyday life. A bottle sits on my kitchen counter in case of burns. Another is at my bedside for the nights when sleep evades me. (I add a drop or two to my wrists and inhale deeply). When I'm traveling, I take it for relaxation and relief of tension, for protection from invasive organisms, for swabbing toilets and deterring bed bugs. A tiny vial is always tucked in a pocket in my handbag, readily available for a multitude of emergencies such as stings, bites, burns, abrasions, shock and to help distressed friends and upset children.

Aromatherapy for All

If Gattefossé is my hero, then the legendary and energetic Marguerite Maury (1895-1968) is my heroine. Maury was working as a nurse in Austria when her insatiable love for knowledge led her to read *Les grandes possibilitès par les matières odoriferantes (1838), The Great Possibilities for Odorous Substances.* This book became her bible throughout much of her life. Marguerite's husband, Dr. E. A. Maury, described Marguerite as having "a scientific curiosity towards research which was little known if not ridiculed by the great minds of the day."[13]

Living in France for much of her life, Maury saw even greater possibilities for the odorous substances of essential oils being prescribed at the time by French physicians in the form of oral, rectal and vaginal applications. While researching olfaction and the effects of essential oils on the nervous system, she discovered that their minute molecular size allowed for easy and effective absorption by the skin. This led her to pioneer the method of external application of essential oils, and in taking aromatherapy out of the medical framework, she brought it to the layperson. She taught her hands-on style throughout Europe, opening clinics in France, Switzerland and England. From my personal experience,

47

the soothing rhythmic flow of a full-body aromatherapy massage, a head, neck and back treatment, or a foot reflexology session coupled with the application of fragrant essential oils is nothing short of therapeutic bliss. Fully conscious of these effects, Maury wrote about the indisputable benefits of healing aromas on the psychological and mental states of individuals in her book *The Secret of Life and Youth*, first published in 1964.

Respect for Nature Returns

Much of the work of the early pioneers of aromatherapy occurred in the first half of the twentieth century. Then the 1960s brought the hippies, flower power, and Rachel Carson's groundbreaking book, *Silent Spring (1962)*. Carson exposed the rampant destruction of the environment that was occurring due to the indiscriminate use of pesticides. Her alarming exposé, which awakened and rekindled respect and concern for the natural world, precipitated the ecology and counterculture movements. Devotees supporting the cause went back to the land, lived in communes, initiated organic gardening, opened health food stores and published the *Whole Earth Catalog*. By the 1970s, books such as Robert Tisserand's *The Art of Aromatherapy* had found a receptive audience and inspired aromatherapy's popularity in England. If it weren't for Tisserand and a core of dedicated enthusiasts who followed, the therapy might have remained a method of treatment practiced solely by the medical doctors of France.

By the 1980s, two models of aromatherapy were emerging. The French medical model carried an aura of mystique. The English model, which emphasized olfaction and the external application of the oils, was user-friendly and more readily available to the general public. However, each direction continues to have its place in health care. As the groundwork for the English style of aromatherapy was being laid, rumours of its beauty, effectiveness and natural approach to healing circulated throughout Europe, crossed the seas to North America and swept up me and countless others in its aromatic allure.

From Folklore to Reality: Aromatherapy Today

Over the past twenty-five years, while immersed in aromatherapy's triumphs and controversies, I've witnessed the misconceptions and attitudes of incredulity directed toward it by the general public, as well as the skepticism of the medical establishment which has referred to it as folklore and quackery. Throughout this period, many of my colleagues and I have advocated ceaselessly for a reversal of the attitude that aromatherapy is nothing but a sweet-smelling, fanciful New Age fad. Now, in the second decade of the twenty-first century, it has defied restraint, triumphed over suppression and neglect, and is beginning to be respected as a powerful and humane form of healing. Its popularity has reached the tipping point I once yearned for, resulting in naturopaths, physicians, herbalists, acupuncturists, chiropractors and other health practitioners incorporating essential oils into their practices.

Aromatherapeutic remedies, so intimately connected with our physiology and psyche, have withstood the test of time. Little did the alchemists know that, by toiling to extract the odiferous principle from the juices of plants, they were providing the future of humanity with the liquid gold critical for supporting its health and equilibrium in an era of overburdened health care systems.

Rosemary
Rosmarinus officinalis

Botanical Family:	*Lamiaceae*
Country of Origin:	Spain, France, Morocco, Tunisia
Fragrance Group:	Top note
Aroma:	Powerful, herbaceous camphor-note
Extraction Process:	Steam distillation
Derived From:	Flowering tops, stalks and leaves
Valuable Uses:	Physical: antiseptic, headaches, muscular pain, bronchitis, sluggish circulation, digestive disorders, colds, flu; stimulates vitality
	Emotional/Mental/Spiritual: improves concentration, mental clarity, memory
Of Added Interest:	Students in ancient Greece wore rosemary wreaths on their heads to stimulate learning.
Contraindications:	Caution in pregnancy; caution with high blood pressure and epilepsy. Best avoided with the elderly and small children.

Fragrant Grace

The ancients believed the soul received its sustenance from the sense of smell. And fragrance—revered over the ages as the "breath of heaven"—continues to play a role in spiritual traditions throughout the world. On my writing table, I keep an old sandalwood box containing recently extracted essences of frankincense, myrrh, cedarwood and rose, aromatics so highly prized in the past that wars were waged to acquire them and bring them under the control of royalty, the wealthy, priests and shamans. While inhaling these scents of antiquity, I'm transported through the fragrant aeons of time like a pilgrim seeking to experience the mysteries of the past and of the sacred.

I start my scented odyssey four thousand years ago in the Middle East in Mesopotamia, the cradle of civilization where recorded history began. The Garden of Eden is believed to have been located in Mesopotamia's fertile plains, and it was here the story of Adam and Eve originated, initiating the three monotheistic religions: Judaism, Christianity and Islam. Over the centuries, the Sumerians, Babylonians and Assyrians populated these lands of lush gardens where botanicals not only fragranced the air but were used lavishly in spiritual ritual. The cedar mountains were considered the abode of gods and goddesses, and from this period came the poem "The Epic of Gilgamesh." It reads in part:

> I brought out an offering and offered it to the four
> directions, I set up an incense offering on the sum-
> mit of the mountain, I arranged seven and seven cult
> vessels, I heaped reeds, cedar and myrtle in their per-
> fume burners. The gods smelled the savour, the gods
> smelled the sweet savour, the gods crowded around
> the sacrificer like flies.[14]

One of the first recorded references to the still and the process of distillation appears on a Mesopotamian cuneiform tab-
let dated 1200 BC. It tells of Tapputi-Belatekallim, a woman
and palace overseer who distilled aromatic plant materials and
prepared medicinal tinctures and perfumes. Some historians
recognize her as the world's first chemist. However, it's the
ancient Egyptians who are considered the pioneers of our civilization's perfumed path. Their culture was redolent with aroma. Using warm oil and crude distillers, they coaxed aromatic
juices from petals, leaves, barks and resins, formulating them
into ointments, perfumes and incense. According to archeolo-
gist and aromatic explorer John Steele, the Egyptians revered
the nose as a sanctuary for the gods and fragrance as a life-giving force. The heart was deemed the seat of consciousness, and
since little value was given to the brain, it was disposed of
during the sacred process of embalming. Essences of cinnamon,
clove, nutmeg, cedarwood and frankincense, valued for their
antiseptic and flesh-preserving qualities as well as for their aromas, were packed into body cavities as preservatives. And elaborate urns brimming with perfume surrounded mummified bodies in their crypts to accompany the souls of the dead on their
journey to the afterlife.

It's likely the five-foot-high stems of Egypt's sacred blue water lily, towering above the surface of the lowlands of the Nile,
created an aura of mystique for the elite priesthood who harvested this exotic plant. From its flower—prized above all others
and considered the symbol of creation—a tincture was prepared
that produced a mind-altering ecstasy and reputedly opened a

portal for communicating with divine powers. Highly diluted preparations of the same tincture were dispersed to Egypt's commoners and ingested as a tonic for good health.

As I continue my journey, I envision wandering through the marbled cities of Greece in 300 BCE. The Greeks excelled in the fields of medicine and personal hygiene, and Hippocrates—a leading philosopher who is also considered the father of medicine—encouraged his country's citizens to indulge in a daily scented bath and a fragrant massage as insurance for good health. The gods and goddesses of Greek mythology played a significant role in daily life in ancient Greece, and the myths from that period tell us they trailed heavenly scented perfumes in their wake, which offered mortals therapeutic benefits as well as sensual delight. The high priestess and Oracle of Delphi herself burned bay leaves to induce her powers of divination for receiving counsel and prophetic predictions.

In early Judaism, as well as in Christianity that followed, aromatics were used on a daily basis as air cleansers, food purifiers, medicines and insect deterrents. On learning how the applications of nature's botanicals during that period parallel my own use of them today, I feel a kinship with the people of these earlier eras. Beyond daily use, aromatic plant materials were equally valued in spiritual ritual. Glowing embers of incense blended from sweet spices, resins, and gums perfumed Jewish altars in the temples. And in later centuries, as Christian priests waved their frankincense-laden censers to and fro, the deep resinous fragrance of the high church permeated their places of worship.

Holy Smoke

Throughout many parts of the world, frankincense continues to be a fundamental component of religious practice, particularly in the form of incense. At one time, it was esteemed as well for its health and hygienic benefits, and modern chemistry is now providing us with evidence as to why this aromatic resin—derived from the sap of the boswellia shrub and grown in the desert regions of Africa and the Middle East—has been highly valued over the ages. The properties making it indispensable as a healing agent are multifold. It acts as an antiseptic, an antidepressive, a tonic, a stimulant, an expectorant and a formulator of scar tissue. More recently, its potential in cancer treatment is being researched. And in spiritual practice, the burning of the resin purifies the air, deepens the breath, calms the mind and elevates the spirit. Considering this extraordinary array of physical, psychological and spiritual benefits, it isn't any wonder that frankincense and the resin myrrh, both prized and coveted like gold, were gifts for the Christ child for assisting him through life.

It goes without saying that in addition to appreciating the function of aromatics in religious ritual, early societies derived great pleasure from fragrance. In fact, during the Temple period in ancient Israel, entire families specialized in the preparation of perfumes and spices. A passage in the Talmud—the Jewish holy book—says that happiness is enjoyed by those whose craft is perfume-making. And in the lyrical Christian psalm, *The Song of Songs*, oils and perfumes are praised and said to bring gladness to the heart.

Meanwhile, the Romans—steeped in the good life and unduly extravagant in their use of fragrance—imported massive quantities of perfumes, resins and spices from the east. Tons of precious plant materials smouldered in incense-bearing vessels during their processions and celebrations, floral waters spewed from elaborate fountains and flowed through canals to scent the roadsides, and Rome's elite citizens immersed daily in rosewater baths.

Whether employed respectfully or brazenly, fragrance was a way of life throughout these ancient periods of history, only coming to an end when Christian clergy determined it was their moral duty to separate spirituality from the pleasures of the flesh. Fragrance—according to the church—was associated with goddess worship and the rituals of paganism. Its only redeeming value was in its relationship to the mystical, to the scents of saints, holy men and women and those favoured by the divine. The use of aromatics purely for pleasure had the potential to lure the faithful into a path of lust and sin, thus was discouraged.

Remedies Protected

The Roman Empire fell in 476 AD plunging Europe into the Dark Ages, a period of disarray which is also referred to as the Middle Ages by many historians. Monks in remote monasteries continued to cultivate herb and flower gardens and safeguard the healing formulas that had accumulated in previous centuries and would benefit future generations. In recent decades, scholars have recognized the life and work of Hildegard von Bingen, a twelfth-century abbess who produced major works of theology, medicine and music. She evaluated and published her findings on the medicinal uses of plants and emphasized the vital connection between the health of the natural world and the health of humanity. Although lavender has been known since ancient times (the first account of its medicinal value can be traced to Greek physician and botanist Dioscorides in the first century AD), Abbess von Bingen is credited as one of the earliest writers to cite this herb, commenting on its strong aroma and praising its many virtues as a healing agent.

This compelling period of history came alive for me during a visit to Florence, Italy, in 2016. I was jubilant to discover that just steps from my hotel was one of the oldest pharmacy/perfumery establishments in the world: Officina Profumo-Farmaceutica di Santa Maria Novella—Office of the Perfume Pharmacy of Santa Maria Novella. Founded by Dominican monks in the thirteenth century, this apothecary prepared remedies, balms, ointments, elixirs and fragrant waters for the monastery's infirmary from the medicinal plants they cultivated in their gardens.

Eagerly approaching the farmacia's unpretentious entrance, I expected a small, quaint replica of an apothecary of bygone eras, yet when I stepped inside, a grand circular staircase led me up to a gracious establishment. High-ceilinged, charmingly appointed salons as large as museum rooms displayed ancient stills and perfume amphorae in polished antique armoires. Counters and shelves showcasing herbal supplements, health-enhancing elixirs, liqueurs, perfumes, soaps and potpourris invited me to linger and exercise my nose. My elation in discovering an example of the partnership between perfumers and pharmacists as they had existed in the old world was far greater than when I had fallen upon a famed Italian gelateria, and while wandering through this olfactory haven, I lost track of time.

Several hours later, with tired feet and senses sated, I discovered a tea-room tucked away at the end of a long corridor. While dipping Italian pastries into a reviving blend of lemon balm and linden flower tea, I pondered whether this grand, upscale version of the original apothecary—now mainly catering to tourists—would have had the approval of the early friars. While perusing the product literature between sips of tea, I learned the Italian state had confiscated the monastery's assets in 1886 and converted the apothecary into a state-owned enterprise. Clearly, it has been updated to appeal to modern tastes. According to the labelling and listing of ingredients, the shop's herbal preparations have remained close to their original recipes, and its perfumes—imbued with naturally grown herbs and floral waters—retain a reputable quality. But I suspected that synthetic aromas now infiltrated the treasured old formulas, cancelling out their medicinal value, and for me the blush was off the rose. Overall, however, I was enchanted and appreciative of the opportunity to step back to a period in time when perfumers and pharmacists worked side by side. In fact, I returned several times during my stay in Florence to take in what remained of the farmacia's old-world ambiance—and to purchase an utterly irresistible rose liqueur.

Perfumery Flourishes in the East

As amber and rose suffuse my west-coast studio, I allow the exotic aroma to escort me to the Middle East in the tenth century. Although European culture had declined in many ways during the Dark Ages, perfumery had blossomed as a fine art in this part of the world. Persian physician and alchemist Abu Ali Sina—more commonly known as Avicenna—had laboured for many years to refine the process of plant distillation. Eventually successful in his striving, he went on to isolate the soul of the beloved holy rose for Islam. As the distilled liquid—the essential oil of rose—entered the waiting receptacle, drop by precious drop, I envision Avicenna down on his knees, thanking Allah. The Arabs have always loved the rose—the quintessential fragrance of spiritual and earthly love. In fact, in Islam, it is said the angels are pleased not only by perfumes worn by women but also by men who display their masculinity and cleanliness in using fragrance. Islamic men extol the virtues of perfume for invigorating their organs, though I presume the supposition originates from a time when perfumes were prepared from the botanicals in the fields and not their synthetic counterparts.

Between the twelfth and fifteenth centuries, Crusaders returning to Europe from the holy wars in the Middle East carried rose oil, rosewater and exotic spices, which they handled as reverently as the holy grail. Then, the arrival of the Renaissance shifted Europe out of the Middle Ages and aromatics were welcomed back into daily life with great rejoicing.

The Holy Rose

According to fossil evidence, the genus rosa has graced this planet for thirty-five million years. As a spiritual symbol revered in both Islam and Christianity, it became the symbol of the Virgin Mary, who came to be called Heaven's Rose or Mystical Rose yet rose petal beads can be traced as far back as ancient India where they were used as prayer beads. Throughout the world, rhapsodic poems and phrases praise the virtues of this heavenly scented "queen of flowers," which elevates spirits, soothes nervous tension and comforts those who grieve or suffer from emotional trauma. Endowed with anti-infectious and nervine properties, medicinal preparations of rose have been indispensable over the centuries as a general tonic for women's issues, including reproduction and childbirth. In many parts of the Middle East, the age-old tradition of pouring rosewater over the hands of guests entering homes, eating establishments and shops acts as a welcoming gesture as well as a sanitizer, and the custom continues to this day.

Fragrant Temples

Paralleling the timeless presence of aroma in spiritual traditions in the west and Middle East, religions in India and southeast Asia have always been highly fragranced. Buddhist temples—known as "houses of fragrance"—are infused with transcendental scents of sandalwood and jasmine. Sandalwood, one of the oldest known perfume ingredients in the world, has a 4,000-year-old history of uninterrupted use, and its sedative, antiseptic and aphrodisiacal properties have long been utilized. Eastern cultures had not been as highly influenced by the Enlightenment as the western world and the distinction between spirituality and sensuality has remained less marked. For instance, it is generally accepted that the therapeutic and aphrodisiacal properties of sandalwood coupled with seductive jasmine offer earthly inhabitants heavenly bliss as well as health benefits.

During a visit to Bali in 2002, I was entranced by the devotion the gentle Balinese display toward their deities through daily ceremony and ritual. In Balinese Hinduism—a nature-based worship—spirituality, beauty and art embody a way of life. A simple altar on a street corner might hold a single five-petalled frangipani stem, its fragrance, reminiscent of orange flower, honeysuckle and gardenia, permeating the air. Throughout the day, processions of exquisitely garbed men, women and children, arms laden with platters of flowers and hair adorned with petals, solemnly descend the steps of the temples—a fluid and poetic pageant.

A Bridge to the Creator

I end my scented sojourn on the shores of the New World. For millennia, the cedar tree—tall, strong and dignified—has been sacred to North America's First Nations cultures just as fragrant cedar boughs were to the people of Mesopotamia thousands of years earlier. The genus Cedrus comes from the Latin "deodar," meaning "god tree."

My community on the west coast of British Columbia is privileged to sit on the traditional lands of two First Nations peoples, the Squamish ("Sḵwx̱wú7mesh Úxwumixw") and the Sechelt ("shíshálh"). Efforts are made to generate communication and respect between them and the Euro-centred culture of the larger community, and elders from either nation are frequently called upon to participate in community events or to perform a sacred ritual such as the dedication of a new building. In turn, we are invited into their longhouses for meetings, celebrations, craft fairs and potlatches. Their rituals—solemn or celebratory—in the community or in the longhouse, include drumming, singing, smudging and cedar-bough brushing. As ordinary time and space is transmuted into extraordinary time and space, a bridge is created between heaven and earth for communing with the Creator.

Holy Anointing

Fragrant smoke imparts a sense of mystery, awe and solemnity to rituals and religious observances, and its ancient symbolism dates back to the pre-monotheistic era. The word incense—from the Latin *incendere*—means to burn, and it is said that burning sacred plants transforms their earthly form into spiritual essence. As the smoke drifts heavenward, its essence is inhaled and absorbed into the bloodstream, where it can influence the body, heart, mind and spirit.

Alternately, oil imbued with fragrance is considered one of the ways grace enters our earthly world and is linked to humanity's search for meaning. Messiah, or "anointed one," is a sign of kingship, and the anointing of kings, queens, priests and prophets symbolizes their being set apart, sanctified or made holy, whether for the purpose of serving a deity, sitting on a throne or serving in a temple. In *Scenting Salvation*, religious scholar Susan Ashbrook Harvey writes that in early Christianity, "the olfactory aspect of the oil was seen to be crucial to its ritual efficacy and to its religious significations."[15]

The Christian church continues to observe the sacrament of anointing, and it brings to mind an experience I had as a young girl. My parents and my sister and I had jostled for position in front of our new Motorola television set, which—though a simple fifteen-inch model set in blonde wood—had the aura of an altar in the living room of our modest home. It was June 1953, and we were about to witness one of the most momentous events of the twentieth century—the coronation of Queen Elizabeth the Second in Westminster Abbey. Though televised in black and white, articulate commentary guided my imagination in full colour through the pomp and pageantry: glittery ladies-in-waiting, horsemen on magnificent white steeds, footmen in red finery, and, of course, a golden carriage. The Queen, tiny, graceful and serene, entered the abbey like a bride, shimmering in an elaborate white satin gown appliquéd with gold.

This was the stuff of fairy tales, and I was spellbound ... until the tale took an unexpected turn in the early stages of the ceremony. The Queen was led to the throne, a simple white shift was draped over her gown and a golden canopy was positioned around her, concealing her and the forthcoming proceedings from view. At this point, it was announced that the upcoming segment was too private to be televised, and the cameras were temporarily switched off. The only sound that came through the blank screen of our television set at that point was the narrator commenting in hushed tones, "This is a moment so old that history can scarcely go deep enough to contain it."[16] The holy anointing. The most solemn and sacred part of the coronation was about to occur.

In looking back, I recall feeling excluded from some great royal mystery though the interruption served to intensify the drama of the event. Many decades later, I witnessed a re-enactment of this holiest of holies in the modern mini-series version of the coronation called *The Crown*. During the anointing, a golden eagle-shaped ampulla containing the sacred royal unction was carried from the altar, and the amber-hued oil—infused with jasmine, orange blossom, rose, cinnamon and musk—was poured into a golden spoon. Dipping his forefinger into the fragrant chrism, the Archbishop of Canterbury made the sign of the cross on the forehead, breast and palms of Her Majesty. The moment of the anointing signified the hallowing ... to make holy.

Following the sacrament—shielded from my eyes and those of twenty million other mortals around the globe—the canopy was removed, television cameras were switched on, and a cloak of gold— the Imperial robe—was draped across the Queen's shoulders. As the final phase of the ceremony commenced, the crown was lowered onto her head, trumpets sounded, and *God Save the Queen* thrice resounded from a thousand voices echoing throughout the abbey. Cheering erupted in the streets, lined for miles with onlookers in rows twenty deep, hoping to catch a glimpse of their newly crowned young queen when she exited the abbey and was paraded through London in her golden chariot. My sister and I, heads held high, mounted the stairs to our room, created crowns out of coat hangers, foil and our mother's rhinestone jewelry, and ceremoniously crowned each other queen for a day.

As fanciful as it may have been to imagine myself as a queen those many years ago, for me fairy tales have never lost their charm. Yet in our present cynical and more complex world, it's easy to lose the innocence and awe that once allowed us to be enchanted by tradition, pageantry and the crowning of a young queen. As well, present-day awareness of the behind-the-scenes reality of such glamour and romance has jaded any myth of living happily-ever-after in a life of luxury. But as shown in the growing interest in eastern religions, meditation and various forms of spiritual practice, it is part of human nature to search for meaning. Maharishis, ministers, imams, rabbis, priests, and gurus alike are hearing that people are seeking something more, yearning to be touched by something higher and to connect to something greater than themselves.

Through my work with plant aromatics, I've been fortunate to acquire a selection of essences comparable to those used in the anointing rituals of the British monarchy for over a thousand years. And while attempting to replicate the coronation chrism, I have inhaled the intoxicating aromas of orange blossom, jasmine, cinnamon and rose, allowing me to return to June 1953 in my imaginings and partake more fully in the concealed ceremony of the holy anointing denied me in childhood. Present-day production and availability of fragrant plant oils are meeting the needs of contemporary people. They provide a spiritual or sacred significance for enhancing modern-day celebrations and ceremonies, such as marriages, births, rites of passage, transition and death. A drop of honey on the forehead of a newborn, a touch of fragrant oil on the breast of a young girl reaching puberty or the abdomen of a woman who has suffered a miscarriage can bring meaning back into our lives.

Meditating on Scent

Numerous opportunities exist for inviting the sacred into one's daily life—attending a church, synagogue, mosque or temple, participating in a spiritual practice, lighting candles on an altar at home or meditating outdoors on the grandeur of nature. Yet while living in a fast-paced world riddled with anxiety and uncertainty, it's easy to become off-balance and disconnected from ourselves and all that brings peace and solace into our lives.

Remaining grounded and centered can be challenging, and I've had to face my personal shortcomings in this area on a number of occasions. One morning while on my way to teach a scent meditation class at a yoga studio in Vancouver, I left home later than intended, drove at full throttle down the highway, searched frantically for a parking space, hauled my teaching supplies out of my car and raced through the streets to make it to the studio on time. Breathless on arrival, I was a pitiful example of outer—let alone inner—calm. But the serene ambiance of the yoga studio coupled with a soft, discreet aroma flowing from the diffuser in the reception room eased my tension, and after a few deep breaths, I returned to a place of quiet within myself. The experience was a reminder to pay more heed to "walking my talk."

Modern-day living has us spending more time than is considered healthy in "freeze, fight or flee" mode—that biological state of arousal intended for emergency situations only. Fortunately, stress-reducing practices like mindfulness, meditation and yoga have become mainstream and are no longer considered to be alternative lifestyle choices. At one time, "meditation" was primarily associated with eastern religious traditions, whereas "contemplation" was a term more commonly used in the west. Both are vehicles for reflection or spiritual introspection, and only within the last fifty years has research revealed the enormous benefits such practices offer for improving one's well-being. The state of deep quiet that results from slowing the breath has been shown to block stress hormones, release endorphins, reduce anxiety, improve memory, strengthen the immune system, increase cardiovascular health, assist focus and decision-making, promote feelings of well-being and inspire creativity. When the popular spiritual teacher Eckhart Tolle, author of *The Power of Now*, was shown the impressive list of speakers scheduled for an upcoming event being presented by a large spiritual organization, he was asked his opinion of the agenda. He replied that the roster of speakers looked interesting but that paying attention to one's breathing—as often as possible over the course of a year—could be more transformative than attending all of their courses.

Meditating on scent provides further alchemical assistance for calming the mind and shifting one into a place of receptivity. Whether practised in the tranquil space of a yoga studio or in the comfort of one's home, setting aside time and life's immediate concerns to inhale scent and journey into one's self for short periods assists in reducing the perennial chattering of the mind. Essential oils— the heart, soul and life-force of the plants from which they are extracted— act as a conduit for making one more open and receptive during meditation. Scent rituals are beneficial for:

✧ inducing relaxation

✧ preparing for a state of contemplation or prayer

✧ experiencing comfort and calm during times of difficulty, transition and change

✧ surrendering to life's challenges more willingly

✧ increasing creativity

Essential Scents

The inhalation of essential oils can be a substitute for the chanting of a mantra (a method practised in many forms of meditation for entering a deepened state of consciousness.) Coupled with deep breathing, they oxygenate the blood and calm the nervous system. Beginning a scent meditation with a brief anointing ritual brings an added sense of reverence and purpose to the experience. Depending on one's intention, a drop of essential oil can be touched on the crown of the head, forehead, throat, breast, or abdomen or any area to which one is called intuitively to anoint.

Since each individual oil will evoke an experience unique to each person, for meditation, it's preferrable to choose a neutral oil or blend of oils that doesn't hold any particular significance or that isn't strongly associated with either positive or negative memories. Essential oils from different parts of a plant can be chosen for specific needs and purposes. For example:

✧ Needles and leaves—fir, pine, spruce and eucalyptus—provide refreshment, renewal and clarity, like a breath of fresh air or a walk in the woods.

✧ Herbs—chamomile, lavender, clary sage—offer calming, nurturing and healing.

✧ Resins, woods and roots—frankincense, cedarwood, sandalwood, angelica, spikenard—strengthen, center, ground and promote tranquility.

✧ Florals—jasmine, neroli, rose, ylang ylang—encourage letting go and induce spiritual upliftment and pure pleasure.

✧ Citruses—bergamot, lemon, orange—cleanse, uplift and induce joy and enthusiasm.

** Scent blotter strips can be cut from watercolour paper or coffee filters.

Fragrant Journey into Self

Choose a quiet setting where you won't be disturbed. Sit in a comfortable position on the floor, a cushion, chair or sofa and keep a straight back. If desired, state an intention for the process you are about to enter into and/or add a drop of anointing oil to a chosen place on your body.

✧ Close your eyes, inhale slowly and deeply several times and surrender all thoughts, feelings, and concerns.

✧ Hold the essential oil bottle or blotter strip at waist level, rotate it slowly and bring it up and under your nose.

✧ Inhale deeply and slowly several times.

✧ Inhale ... hold ... exhale fully ... hold.

✧ Repeat this pattern and adjust to a comfortable rhythm.

✧ Sense where the aroma travels in your body and continue inhaling until you feel yourself becoming one with the scent. Allow feelings and thoughts to come and go.

✧ Stay with this breathing pattern until you feel it has reached a conclusion ... 15-30 minutes is usually sufficient.

- ✧ Slowly lower the bottle or scent strip and sit quietly.

- ✧ When ready, open your eyes, turn outward again, and sit quietly for as long as needed to prolong the benefits of your immersion into scent and self. Take a few minutes to reflect on your experience.

Fragrant Departures

Flowers are in abundance during times of both celebration and sorrow. Heaped high upon funeral pyres in the east and overflowing in churches and funeral parlours in the west, their fragrance pays tribute to those who have departed and offers solace to those who remain. Some religious traditions believe beautiful aromas repel evil and act as a vehicle for attracting the attention of gods, angels or other beings, and in some cultures, bodies of the dead are washed and swathed in fragrant oils to prepare them for the journey to the afterlife. It is said in Islamic Pakistan that five hundred angels sprinkling perfume from heaven gather near one who has died. Paradise itself is described as being suffused with aroma. Saint Gregory of Tours portrayed the Christian paradise as a broad prairie suffused with an extraordinary perfume. The final resting place of Islam is reputed to exhale musk, ginger and amber. And it is said that followers of Buddhism will pass to *gandhamadana*—the fragrant mountain.

My sister called one morning to inform me our mother's health was quickly deteriorating. Since I had heard that smell may be the last sense to leave a dying person, I tucked tiny vials of my mother's favourite essential oils into my carry-on bag before racing to catch a ferry, the first leg of my 2,500-hundred-mile flight across the country to be at her side. Many years earlier, she had supported my venture into aromatherapy, purchasing books on the subject to be better informed. She came to love an essential oil blend I had given her called Peace and Calming that contained lavender, chamomile and sweet orange. When visiting my aging parents in Ontario, I would sometimes spray the elixir above their heads before bedtime as they sat in their matching blue and beige recliners. With feet in the air, eyes closed, and—like little children—trusting me implicitly, they relaxed as the fragrant mists fell softly upon them and ushered away the aches and anxieties of their day.

My mother waited ten hours for me. Arriving at her bedside, I faltered on seeing the frail shell of her former self, once so energetic and engaged in life. Though she had suffered from Alzheimer's for several years, she had continued to play the piano until just a few months prior in the long-term care home in which she resided. Now, her breathing was laboured, her anxiety palpable. But her warm, brown eyes communicated a clear awareness of my presence, and as I wafted lavender under her nose—the sacred mother of essential oils—and asked if she could smell it, she nodded an emphatic "yes!" Three hours later she slipped away. While grieving her loss, I gained consolation knowing I had offered her a fragrant departure; the privilege of doing so was important to me and it held meaning. One day several weeks following her passing, as I sat quietly in my home, a soft, sweet though unfamiliar floral aroma fluttered past my nose, lasting ever so briefly. I sensed my mother's presence and was comforted.

Ten years later, I sat at my father's bedside during his final weeks in palliative care. At 102, his senses were slowly abandoning him. Legally blind, he'd relegated his thick-lensed glasses to the drawer of a bedside table where they lay beside his hearing aids. As I sat with him, his eyes would wander around the room and then fixate on points above my head as though something had entered his field of vision, and he'd utter comments such as, "It won't be long now," or "I'm almost there." To offer him tranquility, and knowing he still loved the scent of roses, I would massage his feet with rose oil. And I sprayed rosewater in his room until the day he took his final breath as the nursing home chaplain read him a passage about love.

Calling All Angels

Thou perceivest the flowers

Put forth their precious odours

And none can tell how from so small

a centre come such sweets,

forgetting that within that centre

eternity expands its ever-during doors.

A selection from Milton, by William Blake

It may never be known whether or not the presence of aroma can assist one's passage from this world. Nevertheless, the deep inhalation of flowers may have delayed the final exodus of my long-time friend Jolanda, and I conclude this chapter by disclosing her experience. An active—and in my estimation, fearless—sixty-two-year-old, she fell off a sixteen-foot ladder while shingling the roof of her daughter's home. During the moments between the ladder's first wobble, its backward descent and when Jolanda landed on hard ground and lost consciousness, thoughts of family raced through her mind. She writes of her experience:

> I find myself walking in a beautiful garden. Flowers almost the size of my height are welcoming me. They are beautiful. I have never ever seen them before, and each resembles an individual personality. This is a perfect world here! The flowers and I can talk to each other, we understand each other and there is absolute peace here. I am in awe of this world and want to stay. But wait. There is also a lovely fragrance and I wonder, is this the fragrance of lilacs? No, not quite. Is it one of lily? To find out I inhale deeply.

Jolanda's next memory is seeing her daughter peering anxiously down at her while blurting out to the 911 operator that her mother was breathing, though her lips had been blue only moments earlier. (Her daughter told Jolanda later that when she found her lying motionless on the ground, she had called out the names of all the angels she could remember.) Following a thorough examination in the emergency ward, Jolanda was found to be badly bruised yet miraculously free of injury, and she was sent home. Many months later, I asked what her experience meant to her and she responded:

I question who sent me those fragrances, making me so curious to identify them that I inhaled deeply and started breathing again. To whom do I address my gratitude? However, it is clear to me that it simply wasn't my time yet.

Neroli
Citrus aurantium

Botanical Family:	*Rutaceae*
Country of Origin:	Italy, Tunisia, Morocco, Algeria, France
Fragrance Group:	Top note
Aroma:	Powerful at the same time light, sweet, radiant floral
Extraction Process:	Steam distillation
Derived From:	Fresh orange blossoms
Valuable Uses:	Physical: heart palpitations, intestinal spasm, PMS, skin care,
	Emotional/Mental/Spiritual: nervous tension, anxiety, fear, shock, grief, stress, tension; spiritually uplifting
Of Added Interest:	Neroli is one of the most precious and costly essential oils. Thousands of pounds of orange blossoms are required to produce a very small amount of neroli essential oil.
Contraindications:	None known

The Golden Age of Perfumery

*P*eople have always been enamoured of beautiful fragrance, going to great efforts to macerate, steep, infuse and distill plant matter to extract its beguiling essence. Yet most of us born in the twentieth and twenty-first centuries have never known the "lost paradises of natural perfumes of the past and of the spirit," so nostalgically invoked by smell researcher Paolo Rovesti in his book *In Search of Perfumes Lost.*[17] Today, much of nature's beneficence is replicated in the chemistry labs of giant perfume houses. From a five-hundred-dollar Dior parfum to a dollar-store toilet water, the formulas created for the hundreds of new fragrances launched each year contain a negligible amount of raw plant materials and I had always found this reality disheartening.

However, in 2004 I read *Essence and Alchemy: A Book of Perfume,* by American natural perfumer Mandy Aftel, and it transported me to the same heights I had experienced during my first whiff of lavender essential oil ten years earlier. The book describes the secrets of the lost art of perfumery, which she had uncovered buried deep inside antique books and reference libraries. I became intrigued by these "lost paradises of natural perfumes" that had been created solely from the palette of plant materials rooted in nature. Until this time, I had mainly been engaged in studying the therapeutic benefits of plant essences, but I was motivated to learn about the principles surrounding their aesthetic value as well. When I learned that Aftel offered a home-study program in natural perfumery, I entered "smell school" once again and began working with bold, unfamiliar essences—galbanum, seaweed, cocoa, coffee and hay—not traditionally used in aromatherapy. And when Aftel announced the launch of her in-studio classes in Berkeley later that same year, the opportunity was impossible to resist. A longtime aromatherapy colleague and I—the only Canadians accepted into that first class of ten students—reorganized our lives and timetables and commuted between Vancouver and Berkeley four times in the following two years.

Aftel's home studio in trendy North Berkeley is a block from the original Peet's Coffee—the revolutionary roaster of gourmet coffee established in the US in 1966, long before Seattle Coffee and Starbucks arrived on the scene. And Aftel's garden backs onto Chez Panisse, a restaurant famed since 1971 for its California cuisine and owned by organic food activist Alice Waters. Overall, the entire locale still oozed the Bohemian ambiance I recalled from the early 1970s when I frequented the original Body Shop on Telegraph Avenue. Each of these Berkeley-birthed businesses had revolutionized their industries and made their names famous around the world. And there I was planted in their midst, an eager seedling hoping to sprout and bloom as an artisan natural perfumer under the guidance of yet another rising superstar on the Berkeley scene.

Budding Perfumers

The scent of aged wood melding with the aromas of antiquity drifting from Aftel's craftsman home studio greeted my Canadian colleague Dorothea and I on our first morning of class. Her magnificent "perfume organ"—the tiered shelves that organize a perfumer's top, middle and base note essences—cradled her fragrant inventory and displayed row upon row of tantalizing raw materials in small, simple glass bottles. I felt like I was a twenty-three-year-old again in Paris, peering into gleaming cabinets that showcased crystal perfume flaçons and teased me to sample. But the comparison ended there. I sensed this new experience would prove to be light-years beyond the lustrous scents of Paris, and having arrived with a voracious smell appetite, I eagerly anticipated the forthcoming olfactory feast.

With trustful abandon, Aftel laid bare her perfume organ of treasured essences and encouraged us to approach and experiment. Under her guidance for the ensuing two years, we learned to be daring in our efforts to create harmonious blends and to take risks in striving for the beautiful. While awaiting inspiration, we were like musicians in front of a blank composition sheet or artists gazing upon a clean canvas. We began each creative effort by evoking an image, visualizing a concept, and determining if the theme of our perfume was to be flirty, elegant, sexy, classic, exotic, or mysterious. Did we aspire to highlight a floral, spicy, woody, citrusy, green, or gourmand note? With beakers, alcohol, scent strips and notepads at hand and noses poised as the instruments of our creativity, we blended our chosen essences into fluid form, drop by drop. Most of our early attempts were disastrous, necessitating fresh starts again and again. The process was humbling, yet joyful and transforming.

The Art of Fragrant Composition

Philosophy and music were fundamental to early nineteenth-century perfumers' understanding of the art of perfumery; thus, they borrowed much of their terminology from the language of music. Creating a perfume can be compared to composing a symphony. Like the notes of music, the scents of individual fragrance essences range from low-pitched to high pitched and in combination, they create chords. For example:

❖ Ethereal, mouth-watering top notes such as wild sweet orange, kaffir lime and pink pepper are comparable to a "first kiss," and introduce a perfume to the nose. If it isn't memorable, it's wise to forego the relationship.

❖ Ravishing middle notes—including rose de mai, tuberose, boronia and jasmine grandiflorum, intermingling with spicy notes such as cinnamon, nutmeg and ginger are the heart of a perfume providing body, complexity and personality as well as imparting warmth and beauty.

✧ Mysterious and intense base notes such as frankincense, labdanum, vetiver and vanilla can be likened to the soul of a perfume. Deep and enduring, they support and sustain the top and middle notes, yet linger longest on the skin to provide a lasting impression.

✧ Not to be forgotten are the provocative animal essences—castoreum, ambergris, hyraceum, musk and civet. When buried deep within a perfume, they inspire intrigue and create a unique complexity.

Modern-day, laboratory-created fragrances are based on aesthetic principles, and their formulation rarely takes into account the therapeutic or spiritual values from which the craft of perfumery originated. Prepared from single-molecule synthetics, they lack the vital force and intricacy present in plant and animal-based raw materials which are more compatible with our human biology. In *Essence and Alchemy,* Aftel writes, "A spiritual process, as well as an aesthetic one, the art of perfumery is at once holy and carnal, spiritual and material, arcane and modern, profound and superficial."[18]

With these principles in mind, I sensed that both therapeutic and aesthetic principles could be in harmony once again, and my intention was to gain the knowledge and skills required for integrating these values into my work. It takes a lifetime to become a perfumer of talent and expertise, and I didn't aspire to gain fame or become the Grandma Moses of perfumery. Rather, I considered myself enormously privileged to be present during the resurrection of an art form, which at one time in history was the foundation of perfumery. And as an educator at heart, I envisioned that one day I would encourage others to marry the wisdom of their noses with the flowers of the fields.

Homespun Alchemy

At the conclusion of our classes in Berkeley, I indulged my inner alchemist and transformed my aromatherapy studio into a mini laboratory adding glass beakers, measuring spoons, droppers, warmers, beeswax, fancy bottles and dozens of new odiferous juices. Like my father whose nose guided him in judging the quality of his ingredients, my nose delved into bottles and beakers and ruminated on scent strips as I tested and tweaked my creations. I rejoiced with each success and bemoaned my many failed attempts, which couldn't be rescued or camouflaged and meant discarding precious, high-priced aromatics down the drain.

Fragrance, like music, is essential to our well-being, and in order to introduce the concept of natural perfumery to my local community, I created a presentation called "Scent Songs." In this tribute to the marriage between music and olfaction, participants are introduced to essences in the range of "top notes" as sweet and ethereal as the refrain of a first violin. To floral "heart notes" so exquisite, they continue to inspire love songs. And to "base notes" comparable to the consoling strings of a bass cello. As the essences are passed along for sampling, each person chooses their favourite top, middle and base notes, which together constitute a "chord." Examples might be ginger, jasmine and sandalwood, or bergamot, orange blossom and vanilla. The chosen essences are then blended, bottled and labelled, and each participant takes away their personalized "Scent Song."

Fully absorbed in my expanded role as a natural perfumer in the field of the aromatic arts, I launched a line of artisan perfumes and became a member of the Natural Perfumers Guild, established in 2006 by Anya McCoy. For anyone with a green thumb and a passion for natural aromatics, I highly recommend McCoy's innovative book, *Homemade Perfume: Create Exquisite, Naturally Scented Products to Fill Your Life with Botanical Aromas (2018)*. A master gardener and experienced natural perfumer, McCoy brings her knowledge and skill to the domain of the layperson, guiding her readers in the basic principles for extracting fragrance from the botanicals growing in their own gardens and backyards. The dedication and trendsetting spirits of natural perfumery mavens Mandy Aftel and Anya McCoy have inspired a new generation of artisan perfumers.

Remembrance of Fragrance Past

One evening, while spritzing Aftel's spring-like *Honey Blossom* perfume into my hair, a memory arose, startling and unexpected. I was returned to the final day of perfumery class in Berkeley seven years earlier where I had experienced a close encounter with the Garden of Eden. My classmates and I—still bathed in the hypnotic vapours of a full day of perfuming practise—were led into the cool air and serene ambiance of Aftel's back garden. In this lush, peaceful enclosure, we plucked figs matured to plump perfection, lounged on garden benches and imbibed the California sunshine. As we relaxed and reviewed our previous two years of class time together, we dipped figs into glass jars of dark, creamy chocolate sauce, one infused with organic lavender, the other with organic jasmine. That sumptuous feast of the senses is superimposed in my memory like an impressionist painting imbued with fragrance. I believe such a restful paradise exists for all who avail themselves of the beauty of life and the soul-stirring aromas of nature.

Ylang Ylang
Cananga odorata

Botanical Family:	*Annonaceae*
Country of Origin:	Madagascar, Réunion, Haiti
Fragrance Group:	Middle (heart) note
Aroma:	Strong, sweet, tropical, balsamic floral
Extraction Process:	Steam distillation
Derived From:	Fresh flowers
Valuable Uses:	Physical: PMS, heart palpitations, hypertension, skin care
	Emotional/Mental/Spiritual: nervous tension, anxiety, PMS, depression, frigidity, impotence; encourages self confidence
Of Added Interest:	Because of its modest price, ylang ylang was once considered the "poor-man's jasmine."
Contraindications:	Avoid with very low blood pressure. May cause skin sensitization. Use in moderation.

Part Two

Subliminal Persuasion

*A*romatherapy's popularity skyrocketed when the millennials, born between 1981 and 1996, started families and caught on to the many benefits of this gentle but effective healing modality. In an era of soaring rates of chronic illness, the millennials were seeking alternatives to costly medical treatments and pharmaceuticals often fraught with side effects. As a result, aromatic remedies have returned to their rightful places in medicine cabinets and first aid kits after a century of suppression, skepticism and neglect. And smell has skyrocketed to rival sight in the senses' hierarchy.

Essential oil sales are on the rise, and diffusers of every size, shape and price spew their scented mists throughout the rooms of homes and down the aisles of stores. Fragrance is "in," it would appear, and the renewed interest in the therapeutic value of aromatic plants and their remedies deserves celebrating. Yet powerful influences are attempting to take charge of our most primal sense in pursuit of profit and control, and the sense of smell itself is not only being taken advantage of but is becoming compromised. This situation poses a threat to humanity's future, and the source of the dilemma began over a hundred years ago when oil erupted in Pennsylvania, profoundly impacting our lives.

Smell Sells

In the late 1850s, oil-spewing geysers prompted an explosion of growth in the petroleum industry, setting the stage for the new oil economy and fueling the military machines of the first and second world wars. A glut of oil remained following those wars, and this is where the story gets interesting. Chemists—the modern-day alchemists—were put to work reformulating the excess petroleum into synthetic chemicals from which manufacturers masterminded a goldmine of products including herbicides, pesticides, heavy-duty cleansers, pharmaceuticals, lubricants and plastics. As large industries grew and initiated a second explosion of growth in the oil industry, their poisonous products infiltrated all areas of our lives, showing up in our food, medications, clothing, bedding and mattresses. The scientific and medical professions put their heads in the sand when it came to demanding research studies on the effects of the new chemicals on people's health and on the environment because it would put them in conflict with the powerful petrochemical industry that promised a booming economy. Though a small number of concerned physicians did initiate the specialty of environmental medicine in 1951 in order to follow and treat patients adversely affected by these toxic products, overall, they were ignored by the mainstream.[19]

Aroma chemicals were also included in the extensive catalogue of new synthetics derived from petroleum and, before long, an unparalleled array of scented household and personal care products was being manufactured, setting the stage for the western world's ubiquitous use of fragrance. The simulated scents conveniently masked the unacceptable base odours of petroleum because, after all, no one wants to smell like crude oil. And the pairing of aroma with desirable merchandise—soaps, body lotions, face creams, deodorants and household cleaning supplies, packaged in new low-cost, light-weight plastic containers, proved to be a winning combination to promote to a booming populace whose incomes were rising. As a result, personal care and household product mega-companies proliferated.

A Little Dab Will Do You

In the 1950s a little dab of Brylcreem tamed my father's thick hair, keeping it sleek and shiny. His morning gargle of Listerine freshened his breath, and on Sundays before church, he topped off his ablutions with a splash of Old Spice cologne. Washing her face with Pond's Cold Cream was the extent of my mother's vanity. The bottle of Yardley's Lavender my sister and I gifted her one Mother's Day languished on her dresser, sparingly used. Nevertheless, a growing selection of personal care products were finding their way into my home and millions of other households in North America. And though there wasn't the same profusion of scented lotions and potions that line bathroom shelves these days, the deluge was beginning.

Snappy radio jingles had been entertaining people for decades, but television's arrival into their living rooms seduced their eyes as well as their ears and further boosted product sales in a booming post-war economy. Smell couldn't be transmitted across the airways, but advertisers had the western world glued to their television sets, feasting their eyes on flashy visuals that promoted an endless selection of products they didn't yet know they needed and at one time could never have afforded. It's likely the ads influenced my father's choice of toiletries. They definitely caught my sister's and my attention. Cheerful models singing and flinging their luxurious locks promised us that sweet-smelling *Halo Shampoo* would "glorify" our hair. We took it to heart, shampooing more frequently while awaiting the glorious proof of our efforts. We bathed with fragrant and foamy Dove soap, kept our laundry cleaner than clean with Tide detergent and chewed Doublemint gum to freshen our breath and "double our pleasure and fun."

It's been said that advertising takes away consumers' esteem then sells it back to them, and it wasn't long before the scented smorgasbord of goods went beyond mouth fresheners, body products and cleaning aids. Shrewdly crafted commercials began advising us that our homes could use a little sweetening as well. I clearly recall Wizard Wick deodorizer's green stick diffuser inching its way up and out of its bottle on the back of our toilet tank.

Its pervasive, pine needle aroma permeated our small bathroom, rescuing us from our own and —heaven forbid— anyone else's odorous effluvia.

For most households, synthetically scented deodorizers were their first introduction to the concept of air fresheners for replacing flowers, open windows or a bowl of potpourri on the coffee table. Even more efficient fumigators followed with the arrival of aerosol cans. For several decades, occupants of homes and workplaces suffered unwittingly under those ozone-depleting sprays of toxic chemicals. Prior to the ban of aerosol cans in the late 1980s, few people had considered that the contents of these cans might be depleting their health as well as the environment. But by then, North Americans had ventured far from the modest dab of perfume on the pulse points or a quick splash of aftershave. They had become intolerant of bad odours and obsessed with scenting their homes as well as their bodies. And as mass marketing escalated, its customers—relabeled consumers—became hooked on smell.

Jingles Jangle

By the turn of the twenty-first century, flashy visuals and catchy jingles designed to manipulate us to spend had grown stale. Jingles were jangling *my* nerves and those of millions of others on the planet. Harassed by gimmicks and bored with visuals, people began muting the media, tuning it out and plugging into seductive tech devices instead. The glory days of TV and radio advertising were diminishing, and ad men were desperate for innovative ways to reconnect with consumers and take back command of their attention. Meanwhile, a solution was brewing in the laboratories of the fragrance industry that would transform the future of marketing.

Scent and the Psyche

Perfumers have always known that beautiful aromas romance the heart and weaken the knees. However, in Europe in the early1980s, aromatherapy—the new kid on the olfactory block—was fast gaining popularity and was asserting that scent could influence the psyche in a multitude of ways. This piqued the interest of the fragrance industry and soon corporate dollars were being poured into smell research, psychologists were hired and olfactory labs, which until then had been poorly funded, were bustling with enthusiasm as a result of the renewed interest in olfaction. Research was demonstrating that smell taps into the primitive area of the brain where—by altering brain chemistry—it can influence mood, memory and emotion. This in turn, can impact sexuality, learning, motivation, stress reduction, and even athletic ability. Of further significance, people respond instinctively to odours before they have the opportunity to analyze their reactions, making the sense of smell the most vulnerable sense.

Such compelling knowledge offered the gurus of the fragrance industry a whiff of fresh perspective as well as a lucrative opportunity for renewed success in marketing their products. A priority on their corporate agendas was determining how they could influence psyches and increase sales by slipping scent into consumers' noses. Soon, shampoos, lotions, creams and soaps, reformulated and relabeled, promised to calm, soothe and uplift our moods, ease insomnia or help us snare a romantic interest. For instance, a cheery citrus-scented dish detergent could deliver us from dishwashing drudgery, and germ-busting tea tree laundry detergent offered added protection for our family's health.

By the early 2000s, anything that could be scented *was* scented, and choosing a product became overwhelming. When shopping, I've always twisted off caps and lids of shampoos, hand creams and laundry detergents to snare a quick sniff while furtively glancing around, hoping no one is watching. But I no longer feel guilty. It's the manufacturer's intention that we stick our noses into their goods so the embedded aromas can "speak to us" and "touch" our emotions. In fact, studies have determined people tend to judge the quality and effectiveness of a product as being superior if they like the scent, believing they're getting more value for their money. Often, when an item is selling poorly, it's pulled from the shelves then relaunched, newly fragranced.

With psychology as the latest marketing hook, smell became an advertiser's dream and a strategy called "scent marketing" was devised. The term is succinctly defined by scent marketing guru C. Russell Brumfield in his book *Whiff! The Revolution of Scent Communication in the Information Age.* Here is an excerpt:

> While visual, auditory, tactile and taste imprints have quite a significant influence upon our behaviour, studies have shown that aromatic imprints (meaningful scents that reach directly into our limbic system from the get-go) have an even more compelling effect on our emotions, opinions and behaviours.[20]

Muzak for the Nose

Smell manipulation didn't end with scented products that speak to people's moods, however. The potential for even greater profits escalated when fragrance companies chose to exploit the fact that since people need to breathe—and breathing can't be easily switched off—diffusing aromas into the environment could potentially engage them beyond their conscious control.

The concept wasn't new. In the early 1980s, the Japanese fragrance conglomerate Takasago began experimenting with scent, diffusing aromas into their factories as a management tool for improving the efficiency of their workers: lemon and eucalyptus for alertness and reducing errors, lavender and rose for calming. Within this same time period, a study conducted by Chicago's Smell and Taste Research Foundation claimed that people were more likely to purchase shoes in a store environment scented with a light floral. And yet another study revealed the revenue from slot machines in casinos in Las Vegas increased by fifty percent when the gambling environment was pleasantly fragranced. By the late 1990s, market researchers were assuring their retail customers that consumers will linger longer when pleasant "ambient" scents are diffused into the air. A pleasingly scented mall or store environment, they promised, would contribute to a favourable perception in shoppers' psyches and result in them spending more freely.

As the influence of aroma on mood and emotions and potentially on spending was confirmed, smell became what some have coined "the communication solution of the twenty-first century." Hundreds of scent marketing companies emerged onto the scene. By 2008, the industry was boasting sales of more than eight million dollars, and revenues were projected to rise well into the billions by the 2020s. These companies and their trained "scentologists" have libraries of scent to suit the branding message of any client—be it edgy, cool, conservative, playful, adventurous or luxurious. Their goal is to create a positive emotional experience for customers, and $25,000 for a custom scent isn't considered outrageous. Beyond fragrancing the environment, some companies are scenting their brochures, business cards and receipts. Embedding a signature scent into a customer's subconscious evokes feelings of attachment to a store, company or brand. Recalling the scent encourages consumers to return for a repeat of what had hopefully been a positive experience initially.

Today, tens of thousands of scent systems are installed in hundreds of countries throughout the world, delivering strategically designed fragrant formulas through sophisticated ventilation, heating, air conditioning and lighting systems. Massive quantities of artificial aroma are propelled into malls, stores, offices, showrooms, sporting and political events, scenting the air we breathe in a deliberate tactic to influence mood and induce spending.

The Sweet Billion Dollar Smell of Success

> For scent was a brother of breath. Together with breath ...
> it entered human beings who couldn't defend themselves
> against it ... He who ruled scent ruled the hearts of men.

Perfume, Patrick Susskind.[21]

Masterminding and controlling just about everything in the world to do with aroma are five multinational corporations: Givaudan and Firmenich, both in Switzerland, Takasago in Japan, Symrise in Germany and International Flavours & Fragrances in the US. Referred to as the "big boys" of the fragrance industry, these

87

companies are in the business of creating and distributing aromas. Tight-lipped and sworn to secrecy to protect their formulas as well as their clients, their factories employ perfumers, chemists and psychologists for creating new smells for a diverse array of clients: large corporations like Procter & Gamble, the automobile and hospitality industries, perfume and fashion houses, major airlines, scent marketing companies, food, furniture and clothing retailers, and big box stores.

Surround Smell

I've learned I'm not alone in feeling accosted by aroma when I enter stores and malls. The odours that assail my nose are understated at times, and at other times penetrate my nostrils unabashedly. Take Cinnabon, for example. The company strategically locates its ovens at the front of its stores, where its message of hot cinnamon buns can be blasted outdoors or down the halls of malls. That smell—I freely admit—tempts me to follow my nose and open my wallet. In another example, when a Dunkin' Donuts advertising campaign in South Korea played jingles on municipal buses as an atomizer released a synthesized coffee aroma, their efforts significantly increased visits and sales at Dunkin' Donuts outlets near the bus stops. Compare the above overt examples of scent marketing with Omni Hotel's green tea and lemongrass signature scent designed to welcome guests with a subtle waft of sophistication.

In the business of scent marketing, it's imperative a signature aroma be congruent with the brand it represents; otherwise, it will be ineffective. For instance, the caviar and champagne fragrance created by Canadian scent designer Tracy Pepe for a five-star Trump Hotel lobby in downtown Toronto suits its lavish interior and moneyed clientele, but it wouldn't suit the chain of Canadian Tire outlets.

Tourism's Scented Profusion

From airline companies to five-star hotels, budget motels, resorts, cruise ships and casinos—in the tourist industry, aroma is considered a major factor in a guest's experience. Some savvy airlines attempt to assuage their guests' travel anxiety by diffusing relaxing aromas at the boarding gate and continue the experience during the flight by offering signature-scented hot towels. On one occasion, when I was waiting in the departures lounge prior to boarding a ferry, I was surprised to detect in the air a subtle ozonic fragrance (a perfume genre meant to replicate a clean marine scent). Could it be, I asked myself, that the ferry company was keeping up with the trend of diffusing scent in hopes of calming agitated travelers when ferries were off schedule and running late?

The smelly ploy of scenting casinos to increase revenue, caught on quickly with all the major players along the strips in Las Vegas. Hotel gift shops in Las Vegas even sell their signature perfumes and room sprays to guests with the strategy that smelling the aromas will conjure happy memories and encourage them to return. I attempt to imagine people's elation in knowing that—with just a few spritzes—they and their homes can smell like a Las Vegas hotel, though I admit the entire concept leaves me wondering if I live on another planet.

Ambient scents aren't confined to retail stores and the tourism sector but extend to other industries as well. Cadillac infuses the interiors of its cars, along with its showrooms and auto shows, with its most recent custom scent, "Dare Greatly." Architects are designing and builders are installing programmable scent systems into private homes as well as large residential and commercial developments. Scent devices are increasing alertness in automobiles and offices, and odour-busting mists fill gyms and health clubs as a line of defence against the smell of "the other." One scent marketing company cautions that it's essential for hospitals, nursing homes and similar facilities to invest in a scenting solution to ward off malodours.

Enter Brave New World

Today, the sweet smell of success is smell itself, surpassing logos and jingles that don't affect us as viscerally. Surround smell is displacing surround sound, and unless one chooses to live in

the wilderness, there's no escaping the oversaturation of artificial
scenting that has become a way of life. In humanity's ancient past,
the sense of smell was finely tuned for sensing and evading predators, yet it appears contemporary society remains under threat
from the predators of our own species who lead us by the nose,
exploiting olfaction for profit. Scent marketers advise their clients
that aroma can lead them to the promised land of fragrant money.

The concept of a promised land is reminiscent of Aldous
Huxley's famed and prophetic fable, *Brave New World,* published
in 1932. The tale, set in the year 2540, tells of a land in which the
genetically engineered population is kept in a perpetual state of
bliss with the aid of a freely available, mind-altering drug called
"Soma." To further enhance its citizens' euphoria, their senses
are sated with synthesized tastes, sounds and smells. And movies
called "the feelies" transmit touch.

Fragrance is pervasive and its daily use is encouraged in Huxley's
perceived utopia. Issues of undesirable body odour are camouflaged with powders and perfumes. Aromas are diffused into hotel
rooms and rotated every few hours. And eau de cologne flows
from metered taps. Aromas also entertain. In *Brave New World,*
Huxley writes:

> The scent organ was playing a delightfully refreshing Herbal
> Capriccio—rippling arpeggios of thyme and lavender, of rose-
> mary, basil, myrtle, tarragon; a series of daring modulations
> through the spice keys into ambergris; and a slow return
> through sandalwood, camphor, cedar and new-mown hay.[22]

Although rippling arpeggios of scent may sound entertaining,
Huxley's aromatic world is alarmingly close to our present-day
proclivity for scenting public spaces. When I'm away from home
and my sensitive olfactory biology is confronted with an onslaught
of artificial scent, I feel that not having a choice about what I'm
inhaling restricts my free will. And I would prefer that no one attempt to influence my behaviour or have a direct route to my emotions. The very possibility of an employer pumping peppermint
into my office or work cubicle—without my permission in order
to perk me up if I appear droopy mid-afternoon—would make me

uneasy, and I'd likely resign on the spot. In fact, for me the whole business of environmental scenting is leaving a bad smell in the air.

Most people remain unaware of the harnessing of olfaction for manipulation and profit. It isn't necessarily the intention of business owners to be shady or deceitful; they're simply following the marketing industry's lead. They're advised that diffusing aromas into their businesses and shops will offer their customers a pleasurable experience that may also relax their spending restraints, and heeding that advice is considered a part of doing business. On the other hand, employing scent to enhance their bottom line isn't something proprietors wish to divulge. They're uncertain whether their customers would approve of having their emotional centres manipulated. In fact, some business owners may fear being accused of subliminal marketing.

Bottled Influence

Since its inception, scent marketing has generated plenty of controversy. Those familiar with the strategy would question whether anyone feels good about being led by the nose. Is it exploitative? Manipulative? Does it cross the ethical line? Many believe it falls within the cloaked parameters of subliminal marketing and could be considered mind control. Subliminal means "below threshold," and according to smell scientists, odours in the environment not strong enough to be consciously detected are still picked up by olfactory neurons in the nose and brain. Therefore, a subliminal scent can be defined as an odour at a concentration below the level of conscious detection but one that still registers subconsciously.

Hidden or disguised messages have been embedded in ads for decades, infiltrating all forms of media including movies, videos and the internet. Hundreds of studies have determined the strategy to be effective. Though not normally visible or audible to the naked eye, ear—and now nose—these messages are meant to influence the mind or encourage the purchase of a product through subtle effects. In bypassing the conscious mind and thereby conscious resistance, they sink into the subconscious, potentially triggering our spending "hot buttons." In other words, it could be said that we are being hypnotized into making decisions.

Subliminal suggestion audio tapes—popular in the 1980s and 1990s—promised to transform our lives, increase prosperity, help us quit smoking or attract a soulmate. I dabbled in the trend myself for a brief period. When one of my longtime reflexology clients, a talented artist, complained she had descended into a creative slump, I suggested that during her sessions, we play my new audio tape of spa music embedded with a subliminal message for increasing creativity. It wasn't something I would routinely recommend to a client, but I'd known Jennine for many years and felt comfortable making the suggestion. As I expected, she was enthusiastic and willing to give it a try. We applied the strategy over a span of six treatments, during which she inhaled a blend of her favourite essential oils—ylang ylang, geranium, ginger and sandalwood. Within six months, she not only developed a new technique in her craft, but she went on to be highly successful in selling her work and accruing commissions. Whether it was the subliminal message embedded in the spa music, the soothing scents altering her brain chemistry, the power of suggestion, a deep state of relaxation, a combination of the above stress management techniques or mere coincidence that contributed to her success, we were both satisfied that overall, the approach had been effective.

Turning a Blind Eye to the Nose

Subliminal marketing is allowed in many countries but not in the UK and Australia. The Canadian Market Association's code of ethics states that marketers must not knowingly mislead consumers, and in the United States, the guidelines are conflicting. The US Federal Communication Commission (FCC) states that it's unethical to transmit information below the consumer's threshold of awareness, yet there are no formal rules, no legislation and no one is ever fined. Besides, subliminal persuasion is difficult to prove, particularly when it comes into play in the area of olfaction. A plausible explanation for this lack of restriction is the considerable power corporations exert over governments. Huxley's utopian world and even George Orwell's dystopian novel *1984* saw a future of government control. Yet it appears that powerful corporations such as Big Fragrance, Big Pharma, and Big Banking have more control than governments in deciding how we think, feel, invest and spend, and much of it is without our consent.

Though scent plays a prominent role in Huxley's futuristic tale, at the time of writing *Brave New World,* he was unaware of the powerful influence smell had on the psyche. However, twenty-five years later, when he published a series of essays called *Brave New World Revisited,* he admitted that although he hadn't envisioned the concept of subliminal projection, were he to write the book again he would correct the omission. Huxley considered it a manipulative scheme to be used on innocent people and he wrote:

> For the commercial and political propagandist ... if he can put his victims into a state of abnormally high suggestibility, if he can show them while they are in that state ... the cause he has to sell ... he may be able to modify their feelings without their having any idea of what he is doing.[23]

Huxley was surprised how many of his predictions became a reality in his lifetime: a massive rise in population, economic power wielded by a power-elite, a decrease in health, increasing rates of mental illness, manipulation of human beings and a love of non-stop distractions. In the years following his death in 1963, his predictions of in vitro fertilization, virtual reality, cloning and antidepressants have also become a reality. Though he didn't foresee the ploy of subliminal scenting hovering in the future, he had been onto something, nevertheless. And now, ninety years later, humanity not only has an excess of available drug options equivalent to "Soma," but we live under a mushrooming cloud of artificial scent—overt *and* subliminal. Unwittingly, Huxley proffered the warning signs. One can only hope they'll be heeded.

Cedarwood
Cedrus atlantica

Botanical Family:	*Pinaceae* (pine)
Country of Origin:	USA, Morocco, Algeria, China
Fragrance Group:	Base note
Aroma:	Soft, sweet woody, camphor-note
Extraction Process:	Steam distillation
Derived From:	Wood chips
Valuable Uses:	Physical: antiseptic, tonic, expectorant; congestion, coughs, fungal infections, rheumatic conditions; fortifying
	Emotional/Mental/Spiritual: anti-anxiety; calms restlessness, balancing, grounding, encourages strength, focus and concentration
Of Added Interest:	Cedarwood continues to be used today as medicine and for spiritual purification, as it was in ancient cultures.
Contraindications:	None known.

The Perils of Perfume

When I find myself withering from too much time online, I pull on my walking shoes and head through the woods and down a nearby trail that leads to a sea-walk. At any time of the year, the salty, green perfume of the sea invigorates my body and brain (and puts those engineered oceanic versions to shame). And during a summer ambling, the fragrant chorus of blackberries swelling to ripeness along the trail lifts my spirits. After a brief half-hour sojourn into nature, I return to work replenished.

My outdoor olfactory experiences are not always so pleasurable. Occasionally, the sulfuric stench from the pulp and paper mill farther up the coast disturbs my sleep when it seeps through my bedroom window. And driving behind a vehicle spewing exhaust fumes raises my ire. But nothing rivals the odorous intrusion I experienced one pristine autumn afternoon while tromping through a mound of musty leaves like a carefree five-year-old. A strong, sickly sweet odour assaulted my nostrils, throwing me off balance and ending my reverie abruptly. I determined the culprit was a dryer sheet fluffing up someone's laundry somewhere along the block. Though I'm well aware of the powerful, inescapable odours emitted by these flimsy, aroma-drenched fabric-softeners, I had never experienced their distressing effects from such a distance. Unfortunately, the problem is commonplace in single-home neighbourhoods as well as in big cities. In my family's forty-story condo building in Toronto, odorous emissions from the dryer vents of multiple tenants are funneled to the exterior of the building only to be recycled back through their open windows with the lightest breeze.

Clothes dryers and scented fabric softeners have usurped sun-kissed clothes fresh off the line ever since TV ads began promoting an array of products that promised sweet-smelling wash, free from static cling and laundry day drudgery. In conversations I've had with others, I've come to realize too few people are aware of the harmful effects of modern-day laundry additives. With wholesome names like Outdoor Fresh and Sweet Dreams, scented detergents and fabric softeners—whether liquid or sheet—pack a powerful toxic punch and can be especially harmful to children's sensitive immune systems. The thin layer of chemical lubricant coating dryer sheets and released with heat is as dangerous as tailpipe pollutants and secondhand smoke. Shockingly, the packaging of these harmful products requires neither a warning message nor a list of ingredients. Perfume and cationic softeners were the only listings I could find on a box of Bounce dryer sheets. According to the health and wellness website Sixwise.com, the odours of chemicals used in fabric softeners are so offensive they must be camouflaged with heavy-duty fragrance chemicals, and its website cites the following harmful ingredients in these innocuous-seeming wisps of paper:

✧ benzyl acetate—irritating to the eyes and respiratory tract; potentially toxic to the nervous system; linked to pancreatic cancer

✧ benzyl alcohol—an upper respiratory tract irritant; potentially toxic to organs

✧ ethanol—linked to central nervous system disorders

✧ limonene—a skin irritant

✧ chloroform—a neurotoxic, anaesthetic and carcinogenic[24]

The toxicity of fabric softeners and dryer sheets negates their use as essential laundry day items, and chlorine bleach is harmful to our bodies and the environment as well. Modern washday habits have veered far off course from those of previous generations who added a quarter cup of baking soda to the wash cycle for softening and brightening their clothes, and a quarter cup of white vinegar to prevent static cling (principally caused by synthetic fabrics). Vinegar also has antibacterial properties. Currently, non-toxic drying options include wool dryer balls that soften laundry and separate wet items, making drying time shorter. Although the wool balls may cost a few dollars more initially, they are good for up to 1,000 loads. Three or four drops of essential oil such as lavender, lemon, grapefruit or pine can be added to the dryer balls to add a gentle, non-cloying fragrance to laundry and to freshen the laundry room. Alternately, three or four drops of essential oil on a small cloth can be tossed into the dryer with a load of laundry. The cloth can be refreshed with additional drops for several more wash days.

Allergies on the Rise

Environmental allergies such as hay fever have always wreaked havoc for a segment of the population. "It's the blooming alders," professes my son who has suffered miserably every spring since he was a child. Now, hazardous and volatile chemicals comprising scented products compound the dilemma of allergy sufferers and are becoming a major health concern to all who share indoor as well as outdoor environments. Lily-of-the valley, lilac and rose, along with hundreds of other synthetically derived aromas surround us daily without our choosing. Sensitivity to these allergens has increased, asthma is on the rise, and people's immune systems are becoming overwhelmed. According to the American Contact Dermatitis Society (ACDS), in 2005, "fragrance mix" was the third most-prevalent allergen in patch tests at eleven-and-a-half percent. In fact, fragrance was voted Allergen of the Year in 2007 by the ACDS.

Presently, at least three percent of the population are victims of a widely researched and controversial medical condition called Multiple Chemical Sensitivities (MCS). Symptoms of the condition include watery eyes, headaches, rapid heart rate, breathing problems, fatigue, nausea, muscle aches, anxiety and depression. The highest-rated substances that provoke the condition include cleaning products, fragrance chemicals, nail polish and hair spray. Yet, the fragrance industry has washed its hands of the entire issue. Assisted by studies from in-house psychologists, it has chosen to ignore MCS sufferers, labeling them anxious neurotics and leaving them floundering in their search for answers. However, other studies are determining that psychological labels and their ensuing treatments—including medications such as antidepressants—prove ineffective for MCS victims. In fact, it appears more likely that depression is a *consequence* of the disability, as is frequently the case with other chronic illnesses.

According to Nneka Leiba, deputy director for research at the activist organization Environmental Working Group (EWG), a large portion of the thousands of aroma chemicals stocked by the fragrance industry are known to be hazardous and are not approved for use. Although companies are required by law to list ingredients on product labels, Leiba reports the law hasn't kept pace with the chemicals in use today. The powerful, multi-billion-dollar fragrance industry is poorly regulated, and bringing a case against it is too costly for the average person to consider.

Consumers are becoming accustomed to scouring labels but are not alone in thinking they need a chemistry degree to interpret the data. One cautionary rule of thumb recommends not purchasing products with ingredients you can't pronounce. For many years, I disregarded the terms fragrance or parfum on a label as simply meaning the addition of scent. However, the reality is disturbing as well as downright deceiving—a loophole in labelling regulations in Canada and the US allows manufacturers to lump hundreds of fragrance chemicals under those terms. This loophole excludes the industry from full disclosure of the hidden ingredients.

Lethal Ingredients in Everyday Products

✧ Sensitizers trigger allergic reactions such as asthma, wheezing, headaches and contact dermatitis

✧ Hormone-disrupting chemicals accumulate in the body and tissues, mimic estrogen, disrupt thyroid function. Diethyl phthalate or DEP—a fixative that makes scents linger—may interfere with hormone function, has been linked to reduced sperm count in men and reproductive defects in the developing male fetus (when the mother is exposed during pregnancy). The European Commission on Endocrine Disruption has listed DEP as a Category 1 priority substance, and the US Clean Water Act lists phthalates as a Priority and Toxic Pollutant, based on evidence that they can be toxic to wildlife and the environment. Health Canada announced regulations banning six phthalates in children's toys, although the use of DEP in cosmetics remains unrestricted.

✧ Synthetic musks (galaxolide and tonalide) are associated with cancer and neurotoxicity. They have been detected in our drinking water and in seven out of ten umbilical cords of newborns.[25]

✧ Petroleum—the base ingredient of a large portion of cosmetics—can generate 1,4-dioxane, a substance known to cause cancer. It is also a kidney and respiratory toxicant and neurotoxicant. Environmental Working Group reports that an alarming twenty-two percent of all cosmetic products contain unsafe levels of 1,4-dioxane.[26]

The fragrance industry has taken control of all of our, or in most cases *their*, perceived odour problems. Strong disinfectants and chlorine bleaches carry names like Floral and Crisp Lemon. Toxic fumes from plug-in deodorizers infiltrate the rooms of our homes, and odour-busting cat litter allows us to exist indoors with our beloved pets. In summing up the dilemma, English novelist A.S. Byatt writes in *How We Lost Our Sense of Smell*:

> "You will sit at dinner and eat your roast, or your delicate pea soup, or your rosewater sorbet and vanilla cream to the

accompaniment of a candle which penetrates every fissure and fold of tablecloth and napkin and nostril with strong incense, myrrh and patchouli."[27]

The Scent-Free Paradox

I'm as guilty as anyone in contributing to air pollution. For decades, my morning ablutions were incomplete without a last-minute flourish of fragrance. Like the American Express card jingle, "Don't leave home without it", forgoing my signature scent was comparable to leaving home unclad.

Presently, scent-free designated zones discourage people from adding that final spritz prior to heading out the door. However, modern-day perfumes are tenacious, and the fallout of last evening's spray can cling to clothes indefinitely. It can be disconcerting to withdraw from a friendly hug to discover our clothes remain redolent of another's lingering perfume. And regardless of whether or not one chooses to wear perfume or cologne, most morning routines include the application of a gamut of scented products in one way or another that include soaps, shower gels, shampoos, body lotions, hair sprays and deodorants.

Unfortunately, diligence in choosing scent-free products doesn't provide the quintessential solution. According to my research, everything has an odour, and nothing is scent-free. Manufacturers of personal care products must either add fragrance or go to a lot of effort to come up with odour-masking chemicals that allow them to promote their merchandise as scent-free.

The marketing methods of consumer product companies are sophisticated and can be ruthless. Through verbal, visual and olfactory cues, consumers are indoctrinated into believing life simply isn't livable if they aren't purchasing the many products that promise to contribute to their self-confidence, comfort, hygiene, self-care—even their success. Companies such as Procter & Gamble are responsible for our fragrance addictions. Their chemists had it all figured out years ago, and the company boasts they have been so successful with Tide's citrus, floral, fruity, scented laundry formula—manufactured from chemicals that have never known the warmth of the sunshine or the richness of the soil—that it has been the best-selling detergent in North America for decades.

Our Genetic Disposition

The omnipresence of synthetic aroma chemicals that arrived with the petrochemical industry has been with us now for over seventy years. It's wise to keep in mind that the habitual use of scented products is creating memories that are based on artificial aromas, not those with their origins in the world of nature. For example, I recently heard of a young man who realized he'd been unconsciously attracted to his girlfriend because she smelled like his mother's Tide laundry detergent. And now, advanced scent technology is usurping our instinctual affinity for the natural world by precisely replicating nature's aromas. However, these synthetic counterfeits will always be factory-generated chemicals and, as such, will never be "alive" or possess the therapeutic and spiritual qualities of complex, plant-based aromas that connect synergistically and harmoniously with the human organism.

Above all, our bodies and minds weren't designed to contend with today's toxic overload that carries biological and psychological implications. In the words of the late American ethnobotanist James A. Duke in his 1997 bestseller, *The Green Pharmacy:*

> Through evolution, our genes have already experienced many of the natural compounds, including toxic and medicinal compounds, often equipping us with mechanisms to deal with the reasonable doses of these toxins. [But] our genes have no experience with tomorrow's synthetics."[28]

The sense of smell and its relationship to our health, emotions, our conscious and unconscious memories is not to be trifled with, and it's time we stood up to powerful corporations. We are fortunate that visionary entrepreneurs have created international databases that assess consumer products and publish the results on their websites. For example, in Canada and the United States, the Environmental Working Group provides ratings for more than

120,000 food, personal care and household products, with more being added continually. The group's mission is "to empower people to live healthier lives in a healthier environment." With their up-to-date research and consumer education, watchdogs like EWG drive consumer choice and initiate civic action to the degree that manufacturers who pay heed to the demand for safer products reap the benefits. They realize their bottom line is dependent on it.

I'm elated to see the shelves of my local stores bulging with environment-friendly, safely scented products. And when I'm uncertain about which item to choose, having the option to consult ingredient and safety ratings on respected databases is enormously helpful. My previous costly stock of kitchen, bathroom, laundry room and cosmetic products has dwindled significantly, lightening my toxic load on the environment as well as on myself.

Geranium
Pelargonium graveolens

Botanical Family:	*Geraniaceae*
Country of Origin:	Madagascar, Morocco, Réunion, France
Fragrance Group:	Middle (heart) note
Aroma:	Fresh, rosy, green floral
Extraction Process:	Steam distillation
Derived From:	Stalks, leaves and flowers
Valuable Uses:	Physical: general tonic, anti-infectious, anti-fungal including candida albicans, sore throat, sluggish circulation, PMS, menopause; skin care
	Emotional/Mental/Spiritual: nervous fatigue; promotes balance
Of Added Interest:	The common variety of geranium used by gardeners does not produce an essential oil.
Contraindications:	None known

Triggers
of the Psyche

Odours are a gateway to the psyche. They touch our deepest selves, linger indefinitely in the underworld of the unconscious and when reawakened, can evoke memories and emotions that influence us in surprising and unexpected ways. Married for thirty years, my neighbour Frank had been inseparable from Carol, and two years following her death he still couldn't bring himself to sort through her clothes and belongings. When grief overcame him, he released pent-up tears in the intimate enclosure of her walk-in closet, where the lingering notes of her amber and orange blossom perfume consoled him. This expression of emotion—of letting go—was essential for Frank's healing and for his readiness to move forward in life.

My friend Laura had her own experience of the intimate relationship between scent and memory. She and her partner Ted had a long-distance relationship and saw each other only once per month. Following Ted's departure, Laura would bury her face in the plush green towels he had used, drawing in long, deep breaths to remember the smell of him. She indulged frequently in this ritual, eventually washing his towels in anticipation of his next visit. His imprinted scent kept her feelings of love, lust and belonging alive.

Laura and Frank's experiences are examples of the emotional portal smell opens into the subconscious ... how memories associated with odour can be spontaneously, often unexpectedly, reawakened. Primal and perplexing, olfaction is wired differently and processed more immediately than our other senses. The olfactory message issued by the scent of Ted's towels would have bypassed the logical or cognitive part of Laura's brain—where her other senses are interpreted—and entered the smell centre, or ancient brain, known as the limbic system. This smell-analyzing area of the brain processes memory, emotion and basic drives such as hunger, sexuality and the survival instinct, explaining why we respond emotionally, not intellectually, to odours.

Strong emotions such as joy, anger, fear, sorrow and shame trigger the brain to release neurotransmitters and hormones into the bloodstream, resulting in a cascade of physiological changes. Anxiety and fear release adrenaline, initiating a freeze, fight or flight response. Other emotions can trigger the release of feel-good neurochemicals such as serotonin, dopamine and endorphins. This was the case when Laura inhaled the odour of Ted's towels. And it's likely that the release of enkephalins—the natural opiate-type pain killers discharged with crying—assisted Frank in easing his grief.

Smell's Code

Turkish professor and perfumer Vedat Ozan has formulated a clever analogy for the scent-memory storing process. He suggests that every time we have an emotional encounter with an odour, a "memory card" is created that enters the brain's smell memory data bank. When that same odour is smelled again, the emotional experience is replayed instantaneously before the logical brain can intercept to decode or interpret the situation. And the stronger the emotion initially experienced in the presence of an odour—whether positive or negative—the stronger the emotional reaction elicited with each recurrence. I had a client who recoiled from the smell of lavender. In childhood, he had endured suffocating hugs from an overly affectionate aunt endowed with a generous, lavender-scented bosom. In contrast, while I was teaching a class of Argentine exchange students about the potency of smell, the zesty aroma of lemons made them teary. They loved the tangy, exhilarating smell, but it also evoked nostalgia for home.

Bread baking in the oven, sizzling bacon, fresh ground coffee, flowers, freshly cut grass and the seaside top the list as some of the western world's favourite smells, whereas garbage bins, drains, body odours and sewers are examples of the most detested odours. Despite the commonalities between people regarding olfactory preferences, each person experiences odours differently. Even occupation and lifestyle can influence choices. Heavily manured farmland or a greasy mechanic's shop might top some people's list of favourite smells and sit at the bottom for others.

Differences of opinion regarding smell preferences exist within families as well. One family member will swoon and wax poetic over an aroma that repulses another. I recall the crackle of cellophane as my father peeled off the thin gold strip encasing his evening cigar. After running his nose along the cigar's entire length several times, he'd grunt with approval before lighting up. I rather enjoyed the aroma of tobacco as the smoke rose and encircled the air, yet my sister considered it distasteful.

The Smell of Fear is Real

Agreeable as well as offensive smells can provoke fear, particularly when they have been associated with trauma. Once an odour memory is deeply engraved in a person's scent data bank as a result of a traumatic experience, it can linger in the subconscious for decades and act as a cue for an olfactory flashback, provoking nightmares, insomnia, anger or depression. If left untreated, the condition can become an ongoing deterrent to leading a normal life.

To cite an example, CBC News correspondent Curt Petrovich—a seasoned reporter with three decades of experience—suffered post-traumatic stress disorder worsened by smell memories following an assignment in the Philippines to cover Typhoon Haiyan. In a CBC documentary, he revealed his PTSD experience, which included his distress on witnessing body bags and smelling decay. "You can't look away from a smell. It's not something that is easy to put out of my mind," he affirmed.[29] Fortunately, he had received immediate attention and treatment on his return to Canada. Experiences like Curt's are common, and strategies are currently being devised to familiarize the armed forces with the smells of war prior to deployment to help accustom them to war zone odours that could potentially lead to PTSD.

In situations that appear threatening, the freeze, fight or flight response is automatically triggered, causing a surge in adrenaline and resulting in an increase in heart rate, respiration and perspiration. This spike in adrenaline can also provoke a less commonly known symptom; fear can alter body odour. I experienced this alarming effect firsthand when a minor flood in my home caused major damage. Highly anxious regarding the financial implications that might ensue due to the necessary restorations, my stress level spiked far beyond my comfort zone. During a particularly distressing call with an insurance adjuster, my heart rate soared, my palms perspired, and my underarms reeked—sharp, sour and acrid. Had the insurance adjuster been present in person, my noxious odour would likely have limited his visit to a very brief consultation.

However, my fetor may not necessarily have been the sole reason for his premature departure. Fear can be contagious. Studies on perspiration are revealing we emit biological signals alerting others to our emotional state. In one study, researchers affixed armpit pads and collected the sweat of twenty novice skydivers— eleven men and nine women—preparing to do their first jump. Underarm perspiration was also collected from these same skydivers on another day while they ran on a treadmill. When volunteer research participants smelled each armpit pad sample, the area in their brains associated with fear was more active when they sniffed the samples from the skydivers on the day of their jump.[30] To further confirm that fear can be detected in sweat, research volunteers at the University of Vienna correctly identified the underarm perspiration collected from women participants watching a frightening movie in comparison to the sweat collected from the same participants while they watched a neutral movie.[31]

Armpit sniffing along with the scrutinizing of sweat under the microscope appears to be the new rage in olfactory labs—a result of the recent heightened interest in the science of body odour. Researchers are now decoding the "chemosignals" that provide clues not only about people's identity but about their physical, emotional and mental health as well. I was intrigued to learn that the skydiver project was funded by the US Defense Advanced Research Projects Agency (DARPA), the Pentagon's military research wing. In his article "The Scent of Fear is Real," written for *The Guardian*, science correspondent James Randerson questions whether DARPA's research means the US military is attempting to isolate the fear pheromone for use in warfare. DARPA denies such allegations.[32] Time will tell.

The Smell of Money

The technology is now available for capturing and synthesizing any odour—including the smell of fear—throwing the door wide open for potential exploitation. I'm reminded of a scandalous rumour that circulated during my aromatherapy studies in the mid-1990s that a credit card company had isolated the smell of fear in order to apply it to their credit card billing. Apparently, researchers at one British company did indeed experiment with this concept by applying a subliminal hint of androstenone—a constituent in male sweat considered to be repulsive smelling—to the bills of a debt collection agency. They found that seventeen percent of those billed were more likely to pay their debt.[33] And to further fuel the flames of hearsay, the rumour may also have resulted from the work of Norwegian smell chemist Sissel Tolaas who not only has more than 7,000 bottles of miscellaneous smells archived in her lab, but she has created scent logos for companies such as Adidas and Ikea. At one time, she was hired to design a scent logo for an undisclosed credit card company that wanted their logo to "smell like money." I find rumoured tales about the shady tactics of credit card companies much more captivating than a YouTube video I came across in which two Australian blokes conducted a sniff test and confirmed that Canadian money smells like maple syrup.[34]

Fortunately, where there's yin, there's yang, and the smell of happiness may also be real. Early results from a study published in the journal of the *Association for Psychological Science* indicates we produce chemo-signals in our perspiration detectable by others when we are happy.[35] Though further research is necessary to substantiate these findings, such an encouraging report would provide evidence for the old adage, "When Mom's happy, everybody's happy."

It's not surprising that the protocol in olfactory research labs demands that volunteers be fragrance-free. It's only common sense that the application of perfumes, antiperspirants, hair sprays, body lotions and the like would skew the results. Such laboratory restrictions offer further proof that personal care products interfere with one's innate olfactory communication system. And considering North Americans spend over one-and-a-half billion dollars per year on antiperspirants and deodorants, I draw what I consider the logical conclusion. Spreading our joy and communicating our fear would be more efficiently broadcast without the use of these products, but it's unlikely this option would sit well with the fragrance conglomerates.

Smell Memories Begin in the Womb

Safe, secure and gently jostled in the warm, weightless sea of the womb, the fetus unfurls like a flower and begins to experience the rich world of the senses. By twenty-five weeks, the olfactory apparatus is formed and fully functional, and it begins to become familiarized with the ever-changing odours both within the womb and perhaps the external world as well—Thanksgiving turkey roasting in the oven or Mom's floral perfume. One day our fully formed fetus separates from the nurturing inner sanctum and is urged earthward. Once plunged into the chaotic world of the senses, limbs are tugged this way, and that, and the infant is surrounded by bright lights, unfamiliar voices, cold air and a profusion of odours. A newborn's first gasping inhalation of Planet Earth's oxygen initiates an intimate, lifelong relationship with smell, that becomes crucial to their survival in this world.

Pediatrics was my chosen field in my nursing career, but newborn babies were my joy. Since I had assisted at numerous home and hospital births, when I learned that Kaiser Permanente Hospital in San Francisco was initiating an innovative Mother-Infant Recovery program, I knew that was where I belonged. From delivery room, to recovery room, to hospital room, to home, mothers and babies were never separated. I loved the work. It was a natural fit and allowed me to be supportive in the bonding process between mothers and their infants. Following the traumatic displacement from the womb, a newborn requires the familiarity of its mother's warmth, breath and heartbeat. Mom's body odours offer her infant comfort and they support the bonding process. For this reason, breast pads, cloths, or pieces of clothing that have been held close to a mother's skin are placed in the incubators of premature infants. And a study on sixty healthy, full-term newborns concluded there was significantly reduced crying among newborns exposed to the odours of their own amniotic fluid. Scent memories had already been imprinted.

Odour memories continue to accumulate in childhood, outnumbering those from later in life. Most are connected with positive experiences: the waxy aroma of crayons in kindergarten, summer vacations around smoky campfires, bubblegum, mud puddles and Christmas trees. A surprisingly large number of my clients have recalled how the smell of Vicks VapoRub evoked memories of being nurtured as children, their mothers massaging the mentholated gel onto their chests and backs when they had colds.

Illness was a rare occurrence in my family. My parents affirmed they were too busy to be sick and instead clung to the views of positive thinking, a popular philosophy at the time. It must have been effective on some level since I was never in a doctor's office, a clinic, or a hospital as a child. But I do have a vivid memory of being a three or four-year-old home in bed, burning with fever and feeling dreadful. A silver-haired woman is sitting on the bed beside me, gently palpating and kneading my chest and back. I feel nurtured, and in turn, I relax and give myself over to her ministrations. Meanwhile, my mother is in the kitchen preparing an oddly pungent though inoffensive smelling home remedy called a mustard plaster. Smearing the thick, warm, yellow concoction of mustard seed, flour and water on a cotton flannel cloth, she wraps it around my neck, layers it with one of Dad's old wool socks to keep in the heat and secures it all with a large pin. In later years I learned the silver-haired lady of mercy at my bedside was an osteopath, an alternative practitioner of medicine who treats pain and imbalance through palpation. Though I'd been ill and distressed at the time, I continue to have positive memories of that experience. Many children are not so fortunate.

Odour and Trauma

Disturbing odour memories from childhood connected to abuse, abandonment, bullying, even medical procedures can resonate for a lifetime. In reviewing my years as a pediatric nurse, I remain puzzled by the psychological mechanism that guards the hearts of medical professionals like a swath of protective gauze, enabling them to work in a field that requires witnessing the suffering of children. I still weep when considering my assigned tasks as a registered nurse—waking infants and toddlers in the dark of night to the cold swipe and disagreeable smell of an alcohol swab prior to the jab of a needle or assaulting their nostrils and taste buds with a mouthful of wretched medicine. Rarely were there a few extra moments in a harried shift to offer comfort.

At that time, visiting hours for parents were limited to a few hours per day, and the comforting presence of a loved one at a child's bedside overnight was not common practice. Tots to teenagers hooked up to machines and intravenous bottles, in traction, or enclosed inside steam tents, lay on their beds feeling helpless. Those too young to understand resisted such restrictions and attempted to climb over the bars of their cribs only to be restrained and strapped down. Others may have felt abandoned in the foreign, antiseptic-smelling environment. My work could be heartbreaking, yet my spirits remained buoyed by the courage and resilience of the children I cared for.

More recently, efforts have been made to humanize the pediatric environment by hanging artwork, decorating walls with colourful murals, piping in music, installing televisions and employing play therapists. Olfaction had remained the most neglected sense in hospitals, but now savvy scent-marketing companies are encouraging hospital administrators to install ambient scenting systems. Such practices seem not only incongruent with the protocol of scent-free zones, but it's difficult to view the addition of artificially derived scents to hospital settings as a sign of progress. While the judicious use of diffused essential oils is employed with success in some medical settings for the benefit of both patients, visitors and employees, their use in a pediatric setting requires careful consideration due to their potential effects on the immature respiratory and neurological systems of infants and young children.

As a substitute, an article suffused with the familiar scents of home such as a pillow, a blanket or a piece of clothing that has been worn by a parent or a loved one can offer emotional comfort when left with a hospitalized child.

The Smell of Danger

Memories of traumatic events can remain in the subconscious minds of children and result in vivid flashbacks later in life. It was a few years before my client Clara felt comfortable confiding in me the full story of her traumatic childhood. Born with a serious heart defect, she had open-heart surgery at the age of four, necessitating the removal of two ribs and requiring one hundred stitches. But this was only the beginning. Had she known what lay ahead and had a choice, she likely would have preferred to crawl back into the safety and security of the warm, weightless sea of the womb.

Clara's first ten years were fraught with illnesses, emergencies and surgeries. In one instance, adrenaline was injected directly into her heart after she stepped on a ground hornet's nest and suffered more than ninety stings. Clara confesses to repressing all memory of the injection. But the recurring traumatic memories were settling into her subconscious, and at the age of twelve, during a routine blood test, she suffered an emotional meltdown that destabilized her dramatically. For three days, her teeth chattered uncontrollably, and she couldn't straighten the arm from which the blood was taken. The reaction surprised everyone, including Clara herself. "I had been the tough kid who never flinched," she told me. Always assuming she was in control, she had buried the stress of her many ordeals under a calm, determined demeanour.

Now in her 60s, Clara has gained insight into her experiences. She realizes the sequence of exposing her arm for blood tests then smelling the alcohol wipes, acts like a lightning rod for the accumulation of the trauma she has endured. Regardless of this clarity, her anxiety has never abated, and she requires medication in preparation for routine lab procedures. "I have to use Ativan for blood tests. I hate being this cowardly. But that smell, it's all over the place—in hospitals, in clinics, in the lab. It's the smell of danger," she says.

A Caregiver's Fragrant Flashback

I carry my own memories associated with odours in the medical setting, but as an adult, not as a child. For many years in my aromatherapy practice I had an aversion to an essential oil called *benzoin* and used it only if its healing properties were a necessary addition to a blend I was preparing. Otherwise, it sat at the back of my inventory shelf, rarely used. I found it perplexing why this soft, balsamic, vanilla-like aroma was so offensive to me until smelling it one day in my studio triggered a flashback. I was a young RN kneeling at the bedside of a distressed five-year-old boy, and a pediatrician was swabbing a section of the boy's upper leg with a russet-toned antiseptic wash. In my attempt to console the anxious child as well as restrain him, my nose hovered above the strong antiseptic. In an instant, the scene and its accompanying odour brought me clarification. The wash was Friar's Balsam—benzoin tinctured in an alcohol solvent. It was used in hospital procedures as an antiseptic wash as well as a preventative against skin reactions from bandage adhesive. Unconsciously, for decades, I had associated this odour with the trauma experienced by many of my young patients during the medical procedures with which I had assisted. That moment of understanding precipitated not only my acceptance of benzoin, but also a renewed appreciation of it. And it has moved up several rows on my inventory shelf.

Inherited Trauma

My experience with benzoin was my personal proof of how odour memories can lie dormant for years in one's subconscious, and I sometimes ponder how my young patients may have been affected by their hospitalizations. Currently, the new science of epigenetics is revealing that memories involving emotional trauma—including those associated with odours—can stay buried beyond one's own lifetime and influence the genetic inheritance of the next generation. In fact, it appears this transference may not be limited to one generation. Through a process called *transgenerational epigenetic inheritance,* information that affects the traits of offspring can be transmitted from one generation of an organism to the next.

Epigenetics means "above" or "on top of" genetics. It refers to external modifications to DNA that can turn genes "on" or "off," affecting how cells "read" genes. Until recently, it was believed that any markings added to genes throughout a lifetime were erased and thereby couldn't affect future generations. But recent research is demonstrating that genes chemically silenced by stress during life may remain silenced in eggs and sperm, allowing the effect to be passed down to the next generation."[36]

The science of *transgenerational epigenetic inheritance* is in its infancy, but early studies are suggesting that through chemical changes to DNA, chronic stress inherited from either parent can impact the emotional behaviour and metabolism of not just their own children but also of successive generations. In his bestseller book, *It Didn't Start with You: How Inherited Family Trauma Shapes Who We Are and How to End the Cycle*, psychologist Mark Wolynn describes how he facilitates his clients' retrieval of ancestral memories and helps them break through inherited family patterns. Wolynn suggests that although our emotional legacy can be hidden from us, facilitating a connection to buried, unconscious memories can lead to a release of emotions. In his work with hundreds of clients, he has discovered that severe emotional trauma experienced by our ancestors that may have resulted from abandonment, pain, physical or emotional abuse, or witnessing the terror of war, may be imprinted into their DNA and biologically inherited by their descendants. For instance, many of Wolynn's clients have parents and grandparents who suffered in the Holocaust, precipitating unexplained emotional and physical symptoms in their descendants such as depression, phobias, fears, pain and illness. Scientists are calling this syndrome *secondary PTSD*. It can occur when people who are in close relation to someone with post-traumatic stress disorder also develop symptoms of the disorder.

Odour Memories Settle in Genes

What I find of particular interest is the recent research on transgenerational inheritance, which pertains to olfaction. It goes something like this: if an odour is present when a traumatic event is experienced, the odour memory from that experience can establish itself in the genes and be passed forward to future offspring. This can result in a re-experiencing of the emotion by one's descendants when in the presence of that same odour.

The theory was demonstrated in the following study with mice (who share about 98 percent of our working DNA). By using olfactory fear conditioning, the study addressed when and how the olfactory experience of a parent might influence their offspring. Before the mice conceived, they were conditioned to fear the odour of acetophenone—which smells like cherry blossoms—by receiving an electrical shock when exposed to that odour. Their pups, who hadn't experienced the electrical shock, also became agitated and expressed fear when that same smell was present—even without the mother's presence. The fear went on to be inherited by several successive generations of mice. A summary of the research paper by authors Brian G. Dias and Kerry J. Ressler states:

> We have begun to explore an under-appreciated influence on adult behavior—ancestral experience before conception. From a translational perspective, our results allow us to appreciate how the experiences of a parent, before even

conceiving offspring, markedly influence both structure and function in the nervous system of subsequent generations.[37]

To date, research on the compelling topic of *transgenerational epigenetics* remains controversial, and its relationship regarding olfaction in humans awaits further conclusive proof. However, epigenetic researcher Bernhard Horsthemke asserts the majority of published studies conducted to date on the theory are technically sound, though they still require independent confirmation.[38]

The Fragrant Mind

The late French psychoanalyst André Virel used fragrances effectively to arouse hidden memories in his patients. And now that it is becoming more widely accepted that odours facilitate memory recall and the retrieval of memories has the potential to address longstanding issues, psychologists and other health practitioners are beginning to employ olfaction in therapy and treatment.

British aromatherapist Valerie Ann Worwood was an early advocate of smell therapy. Renowned for her book *The Fragrant Pharmacy* (1990), she went on to publish *The Fragrant Mind: Aromatherapy for Personality, Mind, Mood and Emotion* (1995). Worwood formulated a restorative system called Aroma-Genera that integrates the sense of smell and essential oils for digging deep into the psyche, and she describes it as a system that uses aroma like a searchlight seeking that which waits to be found. At the time she was writing, research regarding the significance of scent in generating physical and emotional well-being was proliferating in Europe and North America, and Worwood was charting new territory by demonstrating how accessing memory through the sense of smell can influence well-being and healing. She brought her newly developed therapy to Vancouver in 1995 and offered an ongoing series of seminars for those interested in studying with her. I didn't hesitate to enroll.

In class, working in pairs and alternating between the roles of therapist and client, we passed each other scent strips suffused with categorized blends of essential oils derived from flowers, spices, seeds, fruits, woods, leaves, resins, roots and herbs. According to Worwood, each category represents a specific personality type. In practise session after practise session, we inhaled these unique blends and guided one another in the process of accessing and retrieving information from our smell memory data banks. Some students experienced mild responses. Others cried, cursed, laughed or hollered while recalling memories of long-buried issues and experiences from birth, childhood, marriages, family relationships—a diversity of joys, conflicts and sorrows unique to each individual and accessed through the sense of smell. In theory, by re-visiting traumatic issues from the past and talking them through while smelling selected aromas, one can verbally and viscerally change the trajectory of an experience into one that offers the potential for resolution and healing.

Worwood returned to Vancouver four times in the following two years to guide us in this dynamic new process of "aroma-psychology." As novitiates, we felt fortunate to be among its early explorers, yet we remained cognizant that we were trainees in the modality, not experts in psychology, and the results of our experiences in the new therapy remained subjective. Nevertheless, we were eager to dive right in and bring to light unknown aspects of ourselves as well as expand our knowledge of the deep-reaching potential of a therapy facilitated with scent. It is my firmly held belief that doing one's own personal work is an essential prerequisite to becoming a practitioner of any therapy that focuses on exploring or treating the mind, mood and emotions of others.

In practise sessions with family members between seminars, I uncovered unknown aspects of their histories. My dear mother— her face scrunching as she sniffed an agrestic-smelling farmyard blend prepared from the roots of angelica, valerian and spikenard—grumbled about her experiences growing up poor on a farm in Manitoba ... of the disagreeable odours of horse and cow dung, sneezing behind the combine during threshing season, and hot, sweaty summers picking and canning fruit. During the session, she confessed her plan for escaping the poverty of her childhood— study hard at the city school, graduate and become a teacher. My father, on the other hand, well into his senior years by then, smiled contentedly, while evaluating the aromas I slipped under his nose. It was no surprise that the aromas he responded to most favourably, such as cinnamon, clove and vanilla were linked to the memories of the ingredients in his bakeshop. While my husband at the time—an artist—inhaled a blend of floral notes, he sniffed and paused ... then spoke of men in top hats and women in bustles lounging in white linen boudoirs. Still a student in the therapy, I hadn't gained enough experience to discern if he was regressing to an earlier period in his ancestry or was, perhaps, recalling an image in an art gallery. However, in one heartrending olfactory memory, he envisioned himself as a child walking beside his mother, only to have the image suddenly freeze. His mother had died when he was three.

My sister Joy and I, born just eleven months apart and labelled "the twins" throughout our school years, are light years apart in our predilection for aroma. Though a constant light in my life, she expressed boredom throughout the smell sessions I conducted with her. And rarely over the years has she delighted in matters of olfaction to the degree I have. Such differences are common in families. Each child arrives in the world with his or her genetic inheritance destined to be layered in this lifetime with new experiences, which will include a wealth of odour memories. And now, as smell is becoming acknowledged as a potent tool for the exploration of the psyche, the potential exists for delving into the ancestral influences that make us who we are.

Freud's Nose

I attempt to imagine what Freud, the father of psychoanalysis, would have to say about the recent developments in the field of psychology, particularly in its relationship with olfaction. Freud looked unfavourably upon smell's significance on the psyche, believing that when humankind stood upright and became *civilized*, sight became prominent, and we should leave behind any physiological or psychological dependence on the nose. He professed that adults who continued to emphasize the olfactory were arrested in their psychological development. Interestingly, in his book, *The Nose Knows*, psychologist and smell scientist Avery Gilbert

119

uncovered some lesser-known facts about Freud's nose, stating it was "already a medical disaster zone when he hatched his smell theory in 1897." Gilbert suggests it's likely Freud, poor fellow, was smell-impaired from years of cigar smoking, cocaine use, migraines, nasal congestion, nasal surgeries and sinus infections.[39] He may have dismissed Clara's vulnerability and anxiety when confronted with the disturbing smell of alcohol or been disdainful of Laura's effusive attachment to her partner's dank towels.

"Don't it always seem to go that you don't know what you've got 'til it's gone," laments legendary singer-songwriter Joni Mitchell in her 1970s hit *Big Yellow Taxi*. People tend to take their sense of smell for granted, forgetting it's one of the five fundamental ways of connecting with the world around them. And many are unaware that the loss of smell can have serious consequences on one's psychological health. Dysfunctions such as schizophrenia, migraines and very low weight anorexia have been linked to olfactory deficits. And it's common for people with severe smell loss to suffer from depression. Smell psychologist Rachel Herz supports the theory that a link exists between smell loss and depression and she describes it as " sort of a global depression" caused primarily by the bi-directional loop between the olfactory bulb and the limbic system where emotions are processed. "When the olfactory aspect is malfunctioning, the emotional aspect of the amygdala seems to malfunction as well," explains Herz.[40] Such evidence confirming the connection between olfaction and mental health issues strengthens the argument that olfactory testing should be a routine part of medical exams for all age groups.

Italian smell researcher Paolo Rovesti travelled widely to study the psychological effects of aroma on people. He observed that rising numbers of smell disorders among individuals in highly civilized society are well documented, and he concluded that the western world's decreasing ability to smell may be directly related to the emotional and mental stress of urban living.[41] His theory, along with those of the bright modern minds in the new specialty of smell psychology, such as Dr. Rachel Herz, appears to be on the right track. In fact, Dr. Herz considers the sense of smell the *Rosetta Stone* for understanding the emotions. It's likely that psychologists and scientists have grasped a mere modicum of understanding of the effects of smell on the psyche and subsequent behaviour, which leaves many of the mysteries encompassing olfaction yet to be unveiled.

Patchouli
Pogostemon cablin

Botanical Family:	*Lamiaceae*
Country of Origin:	Indonesia, Malaysia, Philippines, Burma
Fragrance Group:	Base note
Aroma:	Persistent sweet, deep, earthy musky
Extraction Process:	Steam distillation
Derived From:	Leaves
Valuable Uses:	Physical: anti-infectious, antiseptic, anti-fungal; skin and scalp conditions; antidote for insect and snake bites
	Emotional/Mental/Spiritual: nervous disorders, reduces anxiety, aphrodisiac
Of Added Interest:	Popular with hippies in the 1960s, patchouli was reputed to mask the odour of marijuana. It is used in some countries of origin and in the import/export trade to repel moths from wool carpets and clothing.
Contraindications:	May inhibit blood clotting and be contraindicated with some drugs. **

** Robert Tisserand, Robert Young. *Essential Oil Safety,* 2nd edition, 2014, page 382.

Intimacy and Identity

"*A*ll of creation was conceived by the aromal copulations of the stars," writes French historian Annick Le Guérer in *Scent: The Mysterious and Essential Powers of Smell.*[42] She is referencing the work of nineteenth-century French philosopher Charles Fourier who had conceptualized the planets as self-created bursts of aromatic molecules. A romantic dreamer and one of the founders of utopian socialism, Fourier visualized a world in which philosophy, poetry and science intersected, and he went so far as to petition the scientists of his day to investigate scent more seriously. To my great delight, his seemingly far-fetched fantasy on the origin of the stars was confirmed in an experiment in the latter 1900s called "Arome," which had been conducted by the French National Centre for Scientific Research (CNRS). In the experiment, a stratospheric balloon provided by France's National Centre for Space Studies had been propelled into space and resulted in the CNRS reporting that aromatic molecules are indeed one of the basic components of the interstellar spaces in which new stars are formed.[43]

I imagine it would have been somewhat unsettling to the dogmatic mindset of the philosophers of Fourier's era when he wafted his olfactory theories under their noses. Rooted in the Age of Reason, it had been their tendency to either dismiss or denigrate the sense of smell. Yet I speculate all of the senses were created equal for assisting humanity in making their way through this world as surely as each of our senses impacts our health, sexuality and spirituality. For millennia, wise women, medicine men, priests and shamans had considered the whole person when treating illness, afflictions of the spirit and sexual dysfunction.

However, mind and body began to be separated in the first century AD when Christian doctrine attempted to deliver the devout from temptation by encouraging suppression of sexuality and any pleasure derived from scent. Further influenced by the Age of Enlightenment, the western world gradually disassociated from the intimate connection between body odour and eroticism. Even the English naturalist Charles Darwin dismissed smell as being of extremely slight service. And to further deter people from trusting their inherent instincts, early twentieth- century European psychiatrists and sexologists believed humankind was evolving from any great dependence on the sense of smell. They professed there was little connection between it and sexuality, though Havelock Ellis— British physician, social reformer and pioneer in human sexuality—reluctantly attributed some value to smell in the area of mate selection. I would have expected that Ellis' insight on the matter might have provided him with sufficient reason for holding olfaction in high esteem, but that doesn't appear to have been the case.

Twentieth-century Western scientific theory eventually recognized that the limbic system encompassing olfaction is hardwired to sexual response, yet when Egyptian smell researcher Raed Rady first arrived in North America in the 1990s, he was taken aback by the general lack of understanding of the role of smell and knowledgeable use of scent in daily life in this part of the world. The rational mindset in the west was slow to catch on.

Smell is Identity

Following you

I threw my heart to the winds.

One day the wind brought me your scent.

My heart swelled in gratitude

And scattered in the wind.

Jalāl ad-Dīn Muhammad Rūmī [44]

The thirteenth-century poet, theologian and Sufi mystic popularly known as Rumi clearly recognized the significance of body odour as not only an aspect of our identity but as essential to who we are. Exchanging olfactory messages has always been a vital means of communication within many indigenous cultures and remains so to this day in some parts of the world. The Bororo of Brazil and the Onge of the Andaman Islands continue to ask, "How is your nose?" rather than "How are you?" The Inuit of Canada and Iceland may rub noses or rub their noses over the cheeks of those they are greeting. In Arab countries touching noses in salutation is the equivalent of a handshake. And in Germany, one of the most belittling insults one can inflict upon another is "I can't smell you!"

And so it is that touching one's nose or lips to the cheek, head, hand or lips of another is a common form of greeting throughout the globe. Hands and faces contain a high concentration of scent glands and it's likely kissing evolved as a means for getting close in order to smell—sharing body odours for the purpose of coming to know or recognize the other. Through close contact with others, the brain deciphers if one is familiar with, attracted to, warned or repelled by the odour messages it is receiving. And just as Havelock Ellis suspected, odours incite attraction and serve biologically in mate selection. According to Israeli professor Noam Sobel who led a research team at the Weizmann Institute of Science in Israel, even a handshake can convey subliminal social cues, since following a handshake, many people unconsciously touch their faces to sniff signaling molecules. Sobel suggests the habit may have evolved as a subliminal means of sampling social chemicals from one another to determine social status, dominance or health.[45]

The Chemistry of a Kiss

Normally, participants engaged in romantic ardour are unaware as well as unconcerned that their biology is simultaneously scrutinizing their saliva and processing a complex series of calculations. In fact, scientists have determined that during a ten-second kiss, *eighty million* bacteria are transferred from one partner to the next. Had my mother incorporated similar scientific data into her half-hearted attempts at sex education, my preteen sister and myself would likely have considered it "too much information" and turned away (though it may have temporarily tempered our budding interest in boys). But like it or not, the tongue is a mad scientist, probing, tasting, evaluating and deciphering chemicals in the saliva. And to further heighten the kiss experience, the lips—the body's most exposed erogenous zones—are densely packed with nerve endings radiating sensitivity. As electrical impulses are fired off between the skin, lips, tongue and brain, the feeling of a natural "high" can result.

However, the master sleuth—judiciously situated above the mouth and usurping both the tongue and the lips—is the nose. While decoding chemical messages in the invisible language of attraction, passion and love, the nose is also evaluating compatibility, determining whether a present partner has the potential to become a soulmate or simply remain a one-night stand.

Beneath the Haze

If smell, our most intimate sense, is a language of nonverbal communication, I question the implications during matchmaking when a hopeful suitor is camouflaged beneath an arsenal of artificial aroma. While swathed in scent, one may never know if a soulmate has passed him or her by.

On several occasions, I was invited by a high school counsellor to introduce teenage girls to the olfactory facts of life along with the benefits of aromatherapy. The girls tended to be timid at first, but as they sampled and sniffed an array of beautiful essences, they soon relaxed and became fully engaged with the topic of smell. Blushing and tittering usually ensued when we discussed the disadvantages of being layered from head to toe with fragrance. I cautioned that an overdose of aroma could be overwhelming, even confusing to the cute guy at the next locker. In fact, camouflaging their bodies with a shroud of aroma chemicals could prevent *his* smell brain from reading and being attracted to *their* biological cues. In addition, how *he* smells may be more important than how he looks when considering Mother Nature's original plan—that selecting one's mate be determined through body odour rather than through appearance.

When each student compiled a list of personal care products used on a daily basis, a litany of shampoos, soaps, body washes, lotions, acne creams, deodorants, hair gels, mouthwashes and perfumes were included. Many of the items were scented with an ice cream shop assortment of artificial fragrances—mango, vanilla, strawberry, cherry and peppermint—and I queried how a compatible mate in their futures could possibly navigate their way through this chemical haze. In addition, alarming studies have revealed that the blood and urine of adolescent girls contain sixteen potentially toxic chemicals linked to the disruption of normal hormonal balance.[46] With this in mind, we discussed the benefits of essential oils, herbal preparations and body products prepared with ingredients derived from natural sources, and I urged them to consider a more prudent use of the multitude of products that seduce them from the shelves of their local stores.

As we continued to talk and sniff, the topic regarding the connection between smell and memory was raised. The girls opened up and shared their personal stories and I was moved by their poignant reflections along with the memories connected with scent that they had already accumulated in their brief lifetimes.

Supporting Our Tweens and Teens

Puberty is a tumultuous time, and aside from painful periods for girls, croaky voices for boys and skin eruptions for both, hormonal changes can wreak havoc on a pre-teen or teenager's emotions. Bodily changes often lead to feelings of awkwardness, anxiety and self-consciousness. For instance, a neighbour informed me that her active nine-year-old daughter believed her underarm odour was unpleasant and perhaps she needed a deodorant. I was uncertain how to respond. Though studies are showing that puberty in both boys and girls is beginning earlier and earlier, it's difficult for a parent to decide whether the underarm perspiration of a budding pre-teen necessitates a drug store cover-up or simply a good daily wash. The topic provides an opportunity for a discussion between parent and child regarding personal hygiene and the changes that come with maturation. Whether or not pre-teens are encouraged or discouraged from using deodorant, I might dissuade a nine-year-old from feeling pressured to camouflage bodily odours that constitute the natural process of growing up.

Young people are under immense pressure from the media as well as from their peers to conform, making it essential for their parents to help them clearly understand all that goes into their bodies and onto their bodies *becomes* their bodies. Education regarding the benefits of good nutrition, and caution related to the downside of scented body products, cosmetics and perfumes is of critical importance. In her book *Renegade Beauty*, Canadian aromatherapist Nadine Artemis cautions, "Beauty is caught in consumerism's spin of acquiring and applying attractiveness with a cash-cow quagmire of chemicals that can't see the beauty of the forest through the trees."[47] Well said. Her warning challenges parents to be creative in guiding their youth in this area, and in attempting to do so, they might consider the following suggestions:

✧ Advise their teens not to be slaves to the media. And why.

✧ Discuss why good nutrition and fresh, wholesome foods benefit their brains as well as their bodies.

✧ Guide them toward products that are free from harmful chemicals and fragrances, including deodorants.

✧ Guide them to take responsibility for their own self care and recommend resources such as the Environmental Working Group (EWG) database and its "Skin Deep Verified Cosmetics Guide."

In retrospect, I wish I had included both sexes in my high school classes. Currently, the redolent efflux of stubble-faced teenage boys is masked by colognes bearing names such as *Fierce, Black Leather, Ultra Male* and *First Instinct*. You can't blame them. Fragrance sales for men have tripled in recent years, and many are marketed to teenage boys. Cell phone ads promise them their confidence will be boosted and their auras haloed.

I have a tendency to hold my breath when passing women and teenage girls in the streets, knowing I may be ambushed in the wake of their scent trails. But I've added men and teenage boys to my cautionary agenda, particularly after having been caught undefended one morning while ambling through a chic Vancouver neighbourhood. A strong fragrance—pleasant enough perhaps but offensive in its pervasiveness—announced itself in its approach rather than in its wake. The fume-bearing offender strutting toward me was a handsome, impeccably dressed thirty-something fellow looking and smelling like he had just stepped out of *GQ*. Steeped in mists of glamour, he attracted my attention but certainly not my adulation.

Billboards, TV ads and cellphones display beautiful people earnestly sniffing their armpits for signs of prohibitive telltale odours. The ads are meant to instill fear that no one be guilty of projecting offensive smells from any orifice or body part. In desperation, some people are taking advantage of surgical treatments to permanently eliminate odour glands and excessive perspiration. The control of body odour with mass-produced synthetically scented products presents an alarming paradox. As these fragrances usurp and replace people's individual body odours and unique identities, their sales boost the beauty industry's profit margins. Western society has come a long way from the days when male folk dancers in Mediterranean countries teased their partners' libido by wafting handkerchiefs soaked in underarm sweat under their noses.[48]

The Pheromone Fad

Each of us possesses a one-of-a-kind fragrant fingerprint that develops to its fullest at puberty and influences who finds us attractive or a turn-off. Individual scent profiles are a combination of odours emitted from the apocrine and sebaceous glands on the cheeks, hair and scalp, breath, armpits, areola of the nipples, anal-genital area and feet. The steroid androsterone is responsible for the strong, musky, acrid odour secreted by the apocrine glands around hair follicles over the entire body and concentrated in the armpits. This odorous compound is believed to play a significant role in determining what attracts us to some people and repels us from others.

In recent decades, the topic of pheromones has created quite a stir in the research labs of the fragrance industry. And rumours of their potential use as sexual attractants have filtered down and seduced the imagination of the layperson. In the animal kingdom, these teasing, biological messengers initiate the rush of hormonal reactions that affect sexual development, physiology and behaviour. To attract the attention of desired suitors, they holler, "Smell me and you can't resist me!" The race to isolate human pheromones is active and ongoing, yet conclusive proof of their existence continues to remain elusive to researchers.

The Smell of Love

Two mysterious little pheromone reception pits called the vomeronasal organ (VNO), which are clearly present in the nostrils of animals, eluded discovery in humans until the 1980s. With the help of a high-tech microscope, the tiny pits were detected to be functioning in humans as well. According to researcher F. Bryant Furlow in his article "The Smell of Love," published in *Psychology Today*, the pits contain olfactory receptor cells that become highly excitable if certain chemical attractants are present. The information is fired off to the brain, speeding past and usurping all other functions. The composition of these chemical attractants remains a mystery, yet the responses reported by a few of the participants involved in Furlow's research is intriguing. Though they weren't conscious of detecting any particular odours, some admitted they had occasionally experienced a "warm, vague feeling of well-being."[49]

Much of the information resulting from the current zeal in olfactory research in recent decades remains inconclusive and awaits replication. Yet sufficient evidence exists to confirm the presence of unconscious odour communication between the sexes. For example, some studies suggest that women who regularly smell men's perspiration have more regular periods, and girls who frequently spend time in the company of men begin to menstruate earlier.[50] Consider the following. A 2006 study at the University of Mexico reported that men are (1) capable of not only determining when women are ovulating but (2) ovulation attracts males. The study, led by evolutionary psychologist Geoffrey Miller, was meant to evaluate the impact of ovulation on lap dancers' tips. Data was collected from an online survey of eighteen professional lap dancers who remained anonymous. They reported their work schedules, menstrual cycles and tip earnings for two months. Although other factors may have come into play here, research findings that represent 290 shifts and 5,300 lap dances—revealed the dancers' tips were highest during ovulation. On the other hand, women taking birth control pills don't ovulate, and lap dancers who were taking the pill earned significantly less.[51]

The race by the fragrance industry to isolate the chemistry of human pheromones shrieks of profit since people believe what they want to believe, and perception sells perfumes. So far, there hasn't been a runaway bestseller, but companies continue to entice consumers with provocative potions for solving their dating aspirations and woes. The majority of the available options are comprised of synthetically derived human-grade hormones—in other words, synthesized pheromones of human sweat. Again, the products being promoted for making people more desirable are cloaking the naturally occurring chemicals in human body odours that were designed by Mother Nature to serve that very same purpose.

Any Excuse for a Party

A scheme for matchmaking using one's personal underarm bouquet so tantalized the owner of an art gallery in Brooklyn, New York, that he hosted a "Pheromone Party." Each guest was invited to sniff a sampling of worn T-shirts, including his own. At the end of the evening, he was introduced to the T-shirt sniffers in the room who found themselves attracted to the scent of his donation to the cause. The concept, originally conceived by the interactive developer and artist Judith Prays, expanded to other cities, including London and Los Angeles. To date, I haven't managed to trace any follow-up reports of romantic liaisons resulting from these events, but I find the concept brilliant. And the attention it's receiving is raising public awareness of the connection between personal odour identity and mate selection and suggests we may want to consider getting back to the basics.

Prior to my knowledge of pheromone parties, I had hosted a more genteel version in my studio called "Perfume Salons," and my guests weren't required to bury their noses into worn and odorous T-shirts. Instead, they were taken on a fragrance journey that highlighted the natural aromatics used in seduction in bygone eras. A sensuous chorus of plant and animal essences including tuberose, patchouli, several exotic jasmines, ambergris and musk were distributed for sampling. Without fail, when the topic of pheromones was raised, it ignited animated conversation. At the conclusion of one salon, Jackie—an elegant single senior—vehemently declared, "I've learned today I need to stay out of my head and go with my pheromones!"

Nature's Aphrodisiacs

The sensual chemical bouquet that has some sniffing the sheets after lovemaking was eulogized by nineteenth-century French physiology professor Auguste Galopin:

> The mutual interaction of odours constitutes the essence of sexual love ... the purest marriage that can be contracted between a man and a woman is that engendered by olfaction.[52]

Galopin went on to reveal his disdain for synthetic scents, warning that heavily scented women not only pervert a man's sense of smell, but also confuse his ability to discern illusion from reality. Considering the fact that the loss of smell can lead to a reduction of libido, there's no denying smell's psychological and physiological influence in seduction. Yet as humanity (and its present-day dependence on synthetic aromas) races at light speed toward the age of robotics, we might be wise to pause and reflect that on a cellular level, our human biology is linked with plants and animals, not synthetics and technology.

Throughout history, flowers have symbolized female sexuality, their physical attributes resembling female anatomy—labia, vulva, vagina and womb. In ancient Sumerian hymns, the vulva was called "a boat of heaven," a vessel meant to carry gifts from heaven to earth's mortals. In Eastern cultures, the lotus flower, pink and plump, is said to be the core of a woman's potent yin essence and represents the sacred life-giving force. Velvety rose petals epitomize passion in the boudoir. No further description is required for the clitoria flower, a plant that thrives in hot, moist environments in Southeast Asia.

While working on this chapter in the spring of 2018, I got a surprise when I turned on the news one day during a lunch break. A radio broadcaster in Vancouver, just across a branch of the Salish Sea from where I live, was reporting on a flagrant example of nature's sexual symbology that was unfolding at the Vancouver Bloedel Floral Conservatory. The exotic titan arum, or *Amorphophallus titanum*, was blooming. Its enormous, ruffled, crimson-lined petals were snuggly wrapped around a six-foot phallus-shaped spike, and as the petals began to open, they exhaled an odorous love call—a stench so powerful it was described by onlooking sniffers as a combination of dead fish, sweaty socks and excrement. Native to Indonesia and known as the largest flowering plant in the world, the titan is also known as the "corpse flower." Its scent is designed to attract flies, beetles and other pollinators which are drawn to the putrid odours of dead flesh.

"Huge Rotten Rare," announced the signboard at the conservatory's entrance. The titan was the first of its species ever to bloom in BC, which made it not only an historic event, but it created a sensation in the city as well. Curiosity seekers—or "olfactory thrill-seekers," as one *Global News* correspondent defined them—lined up for hours for a mere whiff. It would appear beauty is in the *nose* of the beholder since many enthusiasts hung around long enough to pose for "smell-fies." But within just forty-eight hours of its initial blooming, the olfactory spectacle came to a dramatic conclusion. The plant's erect spike deflated, fell limp upon its petals and will remain dormant for many years. Vancouver's titan arum will rouse and rise to display its sensuous aromatic splendour only three more times in its forty-year lifespan.

Come into My Parlour

Sweet-smelling or putrid, the fragrances exhaled by the seducers and seductresses of the plant and animal kingdoms to attract their suitors are composed of a complex blend of chemicals. For instance, the flirtatious and exquisitely scented white florals, including jasmine, tuberose, orange blossom and gardenia, are "ladies of the night." They lure their pollinating partners—the nocturnal insects—into their nectar-dripping parlours by exuding the dirty, putrid note of indole—an organic compound, which is a constituent of human feces and is beguiling in trace amounts. In *Essence and Alchemy*, artisan perfumer Mandy Aftel suggests that although indole may walk the fine line between arousal and disgust, it is a catalyst for attraction.

Humankind's unconscious response to the influence of plant notes such as indole as well as to the glandular secretions of animals may stem from the carnal element that connects us with our own animal nature. Smelled at full strength, these substances are considered offensive, yet in dilution, they are powerful aphrodisiacs and have been used in seduction since antiquity. Normally, pheromones are compatible only between members of the same species, but animal essences such as musk, ambergris, civet and castoreum are exceptions. Each is a cocktail of pheromone-like chemicals considered to have an affinity with human skin and an allure that is awakened through infinitesimal dilution. Dosed appropriately, they roam and meld with other ingredients and can make a perfume "sing."

Powerful and Seductive

Animal essences, used primarily as fixatives in perfumes today, were highly valued in centuries past as potent aphrodisiacs as well as medicines, and they continue to be used for these purposes in some near and far eastern countries. One example is the secretion from the musk deer, an animal close to extinction. During reproductive season, the musk deer drops musk balls produced in two sac-like glands under its lower abdomen and these droppings communicate information to the female regarding the male's genetic patrimony. Few people in contemporary society have smelled this raw, repugnant secretion, yet musk was once the archetype of perfumes, worn by kings and emperors and coveted in Egypt, Arabia, Persia and China. Renowned for its extraordinary healing powers that resolved circulatory, reproductive and fertility issues, musk was also acclaimed for its powerful action on the psyche.

The rare, costly and not unpleasant essence of ambergris, imbued with notes of musk and seaweed, is regurgitation from the sperm whale. Hailed for centuries as a remedy for neurological conditions and revered for its life-restoring lift to the libido, ambergris remains highly prized in perfumery. In the eighteenth and nineteenth centuries, European men rubbed it into their beards to enhance their sex appeal.

In hopes of rousing their lust, some gents of that era also dowsed their handkerchiefs with the fecal-smelling secretions from the civet cat. The best descriptive for this odour is "loathsome." Nevertheless, civet—produced in the perineal secretions of a cat-like mammal native to Africa and Asia—continues to be used as it has for centuries in these same areas of the world as a remedy for hormonal disturbances in women. According to Aftel, civet works its magic in perfumery through its ability "to prowl through a blend giving the whole extraordinary depth."[53] As an added benefit, it is reputed to evoke a respectful fear in others, bestowing upon the wearer an aura of power and strength. This may explain why the small sample I had once ordered from Europe was opened, examined and rejected by Canadian customs officials. Its arrival had coincided with strict border regulations following 9/11 and it is possible its wretched odour was considered suspicious. Perhaps it even instilled fear in the officials.

On the other hand, I had no difficulty acquiring castoreum from a supplier. The North American beaver marks its territory with a thick, yellow secretion exuded from castor sacs at the base of its tail, seducing the females in the vicinity but discouraging other males. When highly diluted, its pleasant leathery note is popular not only in perfumery but also as a flavouring agent in the food and tobacco industry. "Pure animal force," is how French natural perfumer Dominique Dubrana describes this essentially masculine essence. In fact, if a man is hoping to project confidence or an aura of authority, Dubrana recommends he spray his hands with a diluted secretion of castoreum prior to extending a handshake.

Presently, in commercial perfumery, animal essences are derived primarily from synthetic substitutes. As such, they lose the power, integrity and allure found in the secretions obtained from animal sources, though the substitution of synthetics can be considered preferable to the cruel practices commonly employed in obtaining animal-derived essences for mass-produced commercial purposes. Currently, efforts are being made to promote more ethical and sustainable methods in harvesting these powerful, odiferous materials in order that they remain available for cultures that depend upon them for their therapeutic benefits. And natural animal essences are still valued by artisan perfumers who produce their perfumes in small quantities.

The Thoroughly Natural Woman

Today, savvy consumers are concerned about the presence of toxic ingredients in commercial perfumes, and as a result, custom-designed or "bespoke" fragrances created from materials of natural origin have surged in popularity. In preparing them for my clients, I guide them through a lengthy consultation that includes the sampling of dozens of essences. Then, like a conjuring alchemist, I prepare each perfume, drop by precious drop. Depending on the character of the blend I am creating, I may add a microscopic hint of animal force as a final flourish, allowing it to work its wizardry while the perfume is set aside to meld.

However, one might have foreseen what was on the horizon in the fragrance atelier of the twenty-first-century woman. Laura, our lusty inhaler of towels who was introduced in the chapter Triggers of the Psyche, confided in me her latest seductive olfactory scoop. She had discovered the work of Regena Thomashauer, founder of the popular New York establishment Mama Gena's School of Womanly Arts. Along with feminine power, Thomashauer extolls the virtues of the vagina. Through her urging, women are experimenting with the potential benefits of personalizing their perfumes with their vaginal secretions and perhaps, I presume, dabbing a drop or two behind the ears or wherever their imagination might take them. Bespoke perfumes *au naturel!*

Seduction doesn't get more primordial than this. And though Thomashauer's advice may not resonate with everyone's sensibilities, it's an encouraging step toward women embracing their naturally endowed body odours more fully. Too many are obsessed with how they should look and how their lady parts should smell. Women's hormone and functional nutrition expert Alisa Vitti suggests they should have a healthy, musky scent like that produced after a good workout at the gym.

In contrast to women's concerns, modern men fear erectile dysfunction. Television ads promise them that popping a pre-coital pill is all it takes to have them grinning and dancing in the streets the morning after, but pharmaceuticals have side effects. Many of the popular medications used to treat erectile dysfunction are— who would have guessed —smell inhibitors! Side effects can include a runny nose, sneezing after sex, nasal congestion, and, at higher doses, a considerably reduced sense of smell.[54]

Centuries prior to Big Pharma, the men of medieval India had their own equivalent of the pre-coital pill that likely aroused rather than suppressed their olfactory functioning. The remedy, recommended by the fifteenth-century Sultan of Malwa, had them smearing their penises with balsam oil, cardamom and Tibetan musk. The Sultan assured them that the oils, in combination with a diet of fried sparrow's brains, would produce strong lust, erections, flowing semen and a happy heart.[55] In another example of

aromatic arousal that undoubtedly benefited both sexes, the men of the Kaula sect, an ancient Indian ecstasy cult, are said to have anointed their partners with oil of jasmine on the hands, patchouli on the cheek and breasts, spikenard for the hair, musk for the mons veneris, sandalwood on the thighs and saffron on the feet."
56

The Aromatic Couple

Throughout time, nature's powerful and complex aromatics have played an essential role in lovemaking as well as in supporting the health and psyche of women and men. Some induce relaxation; others have aphrodisiacal properties. Overall, they have an affinity for our human body chemistry, enhancing rather than camouflaging our natural odours. For example:

✧ Patchouli, stimulating and provocative, arouses libido.

✧ Ginger, warm and arousing, soothes muscles.

✧ Nutmeg is warming and arousing. MDMA, found in the hallucinogenic *Ecstasy,* was originally synthesized from nutmeg.

✧ Ylang ylang reduces anxiety.

✧ Jasmine, both stimulant and sedative, arouses desire.

✧ Cumin penetrates the senses with its post-coital odour.

✧ Rose Maroc is sensuous, earthy and erotic.

An added advantage of including essential oils in one's daily routine, such as in baths, showers or massage, and prior to, during and post-intimacy, stems from their protective properties as anti-infectious agents. In *Aromantics: Romance, Love, Sex & Nature's Essential Oils*, Valerie Worwood recommends the following Super Protection Synergistic Blend. **

✧ Oregano   3 drops

✧ Palma Rosa   3 drops

✧ Thyme   4 drops

✧ Tea Tree   5 drops

✧ Bergamot   2 drops

Prepare in larger quantities in a small bottle and dilute generously in a carrier oil.

** Essential oils are free from the chemical fixatives which make commercial fragrances pervasive and long-lasting, but it's imperative they be diluted and used responsibly when applied to the body. Application directly onto the genitals and perineum must be strictly avoided.

The Smell of Him

North Americans spend five billion dollars per year on fragrance, yet surveys tell us many women favour a man who smells fresh and clean, like a freshly laundered shirt just off the clothesline. They may prefer he use a deodorant, but a whiff of underarm body odour now and then isn't considered offensive. And a spritz of cologne, though pleasant on occasion, isn't necessary on a regular basis. My colleague Daphne swoons when describing her lover's scent. Brett lives on his boat in the harbour and for Daphne breathing him in is a sumptuous feast of sunshine, the sea, sweat, soap and diesel. Writer Sharon Hale paid similar tribute to the scent of one of her characters and wrote, "I breathed in at his neck ... he smells something like cinnamon ... brown and dry and sweet and warm."[57] The skin of novelist H.G. Wells is said to have smelled of honey. And Alexander the Great—revered for his scent—reputedly exhaled pleasant fragrance from his mouth and skin that permeated his garments, although the aromatic profusion that enveloped him could also be attributed to the chests of fragrant oils that accompanied him throughout his conquests.

The Scent of Her

Men are similar to women in their aversion to overpowering perfumes. Some appreciate a light fragrance on a woman but don't lament its absence. And when it comes right down to appealing to a man's scent preferences, donning an apron and inviting him

139

over for a warm slice of homemade pumpkin pie might score a gal more points than adorning herself with a costly French perfume. Early smell research revealed that the way to a North American man's heart has never changed—it continues to revolve around his stomach. Scents like cinnamon, vanilla, nutmeg ... and perhaps a steak on the grill ... may be the ultimate aphrodisiacs. A hint of lily of the valley or lavender in the air was also shown to heighten the arousal factor of the mix.

We Can't Fool Mother Nature

Although my father was the nose in the family, I like to think I'm a close runner-up. After all, it's generally women who reign supreme in the realm of the olfactory. Our sense of smell is sharper than that of men to the degree that a colleague in my writing group told me that when her children were young, she could identify each of them by their individual odours even if she were blindfolded. Another spoke of her competence in detecting a change in the odour of her children when they were ill. Recent evidence supports such examples of women's superior smell proficiency. A study in 2014 led by Professor Roberto Lent of the Federal University of Rio de Janeiro revealed that although the olfactory bulb is generally larger in men, women have up to fifty percent more olfactory cells in their brains giving them higher olfactory sensitivity.[58]

Curiously, many years ago I was present in a room in which a spiritual teacher from the east was speaking about the importance of a woman's sense of smell. He said that before making love, a woman has the capacity to intuit from a man's scent the appropriate time to conceive a child. Some cultures depend on the sense of smell when choosing a mate. For example, when choosing a marriage partner, the Desana tribe in the Amazon must select someone who smells "different," meaning someone outside the tribe. This ancient tribal wisdom was supported by the work of geneticists in the late 1990s. They learned that Mother Nature programmed women with an innate capacity to discern from a man's body odour alone whether a potential partner will pass on favourable traits to her offspring. They observed that when it comes to reproduction, female mice initially sniff the urine of male mice in order to avoid in-breeding, then choose mates that have dissimilar DNA profiles in what is called the "histocompatibility complex or MCH."[59] Similar tests using humans carried out at the University of Bern in Switzerland bore the same results, except in this study, the women were required, thankfully, to sniff men's T-shirts and not their urine. Normally the MCH segment of the DNA of both men and women allows their bodies to sleuth out alien invaders, making it a critically important biological function when it comes to organ transplants and tissue rejection. However, of even greater significance, the research determined that men's body odours carry important biological information, and women are more likely to be attracted to the odour of men whose MCH profiles are the most varied from their own, meaning their offspring will have stronger immune systems and be better equipped to ward off disease.[60] [61]

In connection with the above research, studies at the University of Liverpool have revealed that women taking oral contraceptives are more likely to choose men with similar rather than dissimilar MCH profiles. Since the birth control pill is comprised of synthetic hormones that prevent a woman from ovulating, they fool the body into believing it is pregnant. In doing so, it changes a woman's body chemistry and interferes with innate attraction and mate selection tendencies so intimately connected with the sense of smell.[62] In fact, when a woman ceases to take birth control pills, she may complain about experiencing an aversion to the smell of her husband or partner, which can potentially lead to relationship problems.[63]

Such research is controversial, highly charged and remains ongoing due to a lack of congruence among researchers. However, a general consensus supports the theory that humans *are* able to discriminate the MCH type of potential mates through odour cues and may unconsciously use such information when selecting a mate.

The western world's rejection, dismissal and concealment of naturally occurring body odours requires reconsideration. We pride ourselves on being an advanced society, yet in all our cleverness, it might benefit us, modern mortals, to acknowledge the wisdom of earlier cultures that acknowledged and respected body odour as a powerful influence in human relationships, sexual development and behaviour.

Jasmine
Jasmine officinale

Botanical Family:	*Oleaceae*
Country of Origin:	France, Morocco, China, Egypt, India, Algeria
Fragrance Group:	Middle (heart) note
Aroma:	Exotic, sweet, honey-like, tenacious floral
Extraction Process:	Enfleurage; solvent extraction; CO2 extraction
Derived From:	Flowers
Valuable Uses:	Physical: antiseptic, fertility, child-birth preparation, menopause, PMS, dysmenorrhea
	Emotional/Mental/Spiritual: tension relief, post-natal depression, stress-related conditions, aphrodisiac
Of Added Interest:	Jasmine is considered "the King of Flowers" and is useful in both men's and women's perfumes. As one of the more costly and precious aromatic materials, its flowers must be picked prior to sunrise before the fragrance evaporates.
Contraindications:	None known

Part Three

The Fragrant Future

Our noses are compulsory to our survival yet have never before in history come under such threat as they have in the twenty-first century. Aromas of the natural world have been usurped and replaced with artificial substitutes, smell manipulation interferes with our freedom to choose what we inhale into our bodies and our brains, and electronic noses—or e-noses—are taking over some of our smell functions. Science fiction writers have gone so far as to prophesize a nose-less future for humanity. Though it's unlikely I'll witness such dramatic change in my lifetime, I bewail any consideration of our noses becoming redundant. The very presumption holds a bitter fragrance and, in my view, would necessitate redefining humanity.

For now, our nostrils and noses remain intact, yet considering the rampant change occurring in olfactory technology, it's becoming easier to contemplate the possibility of a nostril-free future. The more dependent we become on smelling devices the more likely it is they'll usurp our human proclivity for discriminating between odours or recognizing when something "smells off" in our food, our homes, our environment, ourselves and others. This chapter will examine some examples of recent advances that are already being implemented in smell technology though are not as yet common knowledge, as well as a few startling concepts that are on the horizon. Some of the new approaches may sound appealing, some amusing. Others may raise concern and be incongruent with the concept of the future we prefer to envision for ourselves and future generations.

As advances in technology push the boundaries of our human capabilities, all of our senses are becoming revolutionized. Imitation is everywhere, and it's becoming increasingly difficult to discern reality from counterfeit. For example:

✧ Electronic synthesizers simulate the sounds of instruments.

✧ Visual images are airbrushed and skewed until we can no longer discern what's real.

✧ Virtual reality and love dolls replace the intimacy of human contact.

✧ Artificial fragrances, flavours, and colours rev up the smell, taste and appearance of food.

✧ Synthetic scents envelop our bodies, surround us in our homes, offices, malls and meeting rooms.

The present generation of children has difficulty discriminating between naturally occurring flavours and aromas and their synthetic substitutes, and they struggle when asked to choose the taste of real strawberries. Sociologist and modern philosopher Jean Baudrillard expressed his assessment of this current dilemma when he wrote that "the world has come to be completely catalogued and analyzed and then artificially revised as real."[64]

A technology developed in the 1980s called Headspace transformed the fragrance industry by making possible the replication of any scent. Chemists are now able to capture aromatic compounds in the air surrounding flowers, fruits, herbs and other materials, analyze the trapped air, and reproduce the aromas synthetically as well as precisely. More recently, perfumers have adopted a soft extraction method that was originally designed for their counterpart, the flavours industry. In this technique, chemists capture and analyze scent by running carbon dioxide over living materials.

When Is a Rose Still a Rose?

In my world of aromatic indulgence, little can surpass the hypnotic, honey-sweet fragrance of a rose garden. Beloved throughout the world, roses are one of the most biologically complex flowers and are comprised of over 400 chemical constituents, many of which remain unidentified. Thousands of pounds of rose petals are required to produce a very small quantity of pure rose essential oil. The extracted essence is a precious and costly commodity; therefore, when compounding a fragrance blend, companies can get away with adding only a drop of authentic rose oil to "the juice"— as it's called in the industry—and promote the resulting product as containing pure rose oil. They aren't required to explain they have extended the rose fragrance by adding synthetic aroma chemicals produced in a lab. As a result, today, when people are asked for their preference, the majority will choose the synthetic fragrance over authentic rose oil because it's what they have become accustomed to throughout the past century.

And then there's taste, which is highly dependent on smell. At the peak of summer, when I bite into a ripe, locally grown peach and imbibe its sweetness and delicate fragrance as its juices stream down my arms, I'm seized by memories of intense joy as I recall the childhood summers that offered an abundance of fresh fruit harvested from Ontario orchards. In such moments I'm reminded of how food was originally ordained to look, smell and taste. Now the bulk of commercial fruits and vegetables available in the produce section of grocery stores are picked prior to ripeness in order to withstand storage and long transportation hauls. Unfortunately, ripening in transit deprives fresh produce of its intrinsic aroma as well as its taste.

Meanwhile, flavourists in the fragrance and flavour industry have their own agenda and have been manipulating the taste of food since the late 1800s when it was discovered that essential oils could be added to foods to boost their appeal. At least nature remained present in that equation, and to this day, food-grade essential oils continue to be added to enhance the flavour of many processed foods and beverages. However, the concept of artificial flavour was masterminded in the late 1800s not only for enhancing natural flavours but also for replacing them. Now, "flavourists" in the trade flaunt their expertise as being superior to that of Mother Nature, boasting they can manipulate our food to smell and taste even better than it did in its original state. And they do so regardless of the fact that government regulators lack sufficient evidence to assure consumers that artificial flavours and fragrances don't cause hazardous, long-term effects on the health of human beings and animals. As a result, recent generations have become accustomed to strong, synthetic flavours, which they are not likely to give up despite the trend toward adopting a more natural diet and healthier lifestyle. The authors of *Aroma: The Cultural History of Smell* write:

> For all those born into this new world of designer flavours, the scents and savours of dinner will often originate not in nature but in laboratory vials numbered and stored in an industrial flavour bank.[65]

Life Circa 2030

Unsurprisingly, the fragrance industry was one of the first areas of commerce to make use of the e-nose, employing it in the early 1990s for protecting patents and assessing quality control. Yet as olfaction continues its ascent as the superstar of the information era, the fragrance industry is powerfully influencing the future by determining how patented odour chemicals can influence our lives—from the boardroom to the bedroom.

I visualize the future smelling something like the following hypothetical scenario for a young woman I'll call Sarah. At seven AM, Sarah's alarm clock triggers her customized home scent-conditioning-system into action, along with her coffee percolator. Simulated scents of basil and lemon—meant to jump-start her brain—flow through vents in her bedroom ceiling as molecules of mocha java waft from the kitchen, tease her nostrils and coax her out of bed. A refreshing grapefruit and lime body wash spewing from the showerhead and accessorized with upbeat music completes her morning ritual.

Sarah slips a triple-mint "Stay Alert" scent filter into her car's scent-diffuser before pulling out of her condo's garage. On arrival at her downtown office building, customized aromas suffuse the elevators and the offices of each floor. The creativity blend dispersed by her employer—an advertising agency—differs from the crisp scent flowing through the cubicles of the accounting office on the floor below. Or the factory across the street. Seduced by the lure of a myriad of odours in the underground mall at lunchtime, Sarah is likely to make an unintended purchase. For instance, one day, she gives the sales clerk at a perfume kiosk a sample of her saliva and answers a questionnaire about her fragrance preferences. Her pricey new customized perfume is ready for pick-up the following day.

At the end of her workday and arduous commute, Sarah arrives home and relaxes in her home spa surrounded by the sounds and scents of the tropics. Wrapped in a fragrant heated bath towel, she pops a frozen dinner into the microwave, settles back onto plump cushions and disappears into her virtual reality entertainment system, enhanced with aroma. Meanwhile, a soothing, pre-programmed sleep blend comprised of synthetic lavender and rose infuses her bedroom as another fragrance-filled day comes to a close. Such post-modern conveniences are routine for the more privileged population of Sarah's era. By all appearances, life is good. But being confined in a hermetically sealed, simulated scent environment, whether at home or in an office, isn't everyone's idea of the good life.

Inhaling the Action

Like most people, I value my leisure time, which includes an occasional outing at the movies. The familiar aroma of popcorn seduces my nostrils every time, and I usually load up with a jumbo bag dripping with extra butter. However, there's a good chance that one day soon, we'll be smelling a lot more than popcorn at our local theatres. Since the early days of filmmaking in Hollywood, entrepreneurs have envisioned movie-goers smelling as well as viewing the action, but the majority of early attempts at the new technology were unsuccessful and had to be aborted. In his book, *What the Nose Knows,* smell scientist Avery Gilbert presents an amusing historical romp through the blunders and bouquets of these early days of the "scentertainment" craze. For example, he cites the creative entrepreneurship devised in 1929 by the manager of a movie theatre in Boston who poured a pint of lilac essence into the theatre's ventilation system to coincide with the opening scene of a film called "Lilac Time." [66]

The fad for entertaining movie-goers with scented films continued throughout the early half of the twentieth century, and it became even more challenging when efforts were made to diffuse a stream of aromas to coincide with ongoing scenes. The olfactory innovators didn't take into consideration that odours tend to linger in the air and as a result, the flow of multiple layers of aroma didn't always match up with the scenes with which they were meant to coincide. I would suspect the lingering odour of a bunch of dusty, sweaty cowboys wouldn't prove appropriate if it encroached upon a love scene featuring the lead actor and his glamorous heroine. In some instances, theatres remained drenched with a crossover of odours that couldn't be eliminated for days. Not only did the technology never take off, but according to Gilbert, a company called Smell-O-Vision made the *New York Times'* list of the *100 Worst Ideas of the Century.*[67]

Despite failures in the past, the concept of aroma at the movies refuses to fade. Inventors and entrepreneurs continue to refine the technology, and patent applications are processed regularly. In the meantime, some films offer scratch-n-sniff cards that at least offer movie-goers the option to sniff or not to sniff along with the plot. Though I'm curious to experience smell viewing, I don't eagerly anticipate the coming era when a multiple array of artificial aromas will shift between scenes. I might tolerate the dispersal of a ginger and lime cologne that provides a clue for identifying the leading suspect in a spy thriller, but contending with the sulphurous smell of gunpowder would detract from my viewing pleasure.

Beyond Scentertainment

Like it or not, there's a good possibility the "smellies" will one day arrive at a theatre near you. And in all probability, odours will one day coexist alongside visuals and soundtracks in television, home entertainment, virtual reality systems and gaming. But that's not the half of it. The transmission of smell across cyberspace is also travelling toward us at light speed. Minute cartridges containing olfactive information can produce thousands of odour signals that may one day be transmitted through emails, text messages, Facebook, Twitter, Instagram and online ads, making olfactory communication commonplace. To date, attempts at transmitting the nascent technology haven't been successful or well-received, but efforts to refine it continue.

I don't attempt to keep up with the current trends in technology. In fact, I'm one of a rare breed of people who is determined to keep a landline in my home, and while away from home, I carry an outmoded cell phone for emergency use only. However, with the digital scent era upon us, if I don't get "up to sniff" with my devices, I could miss out on the dawn of the cyberscent revolution when aroma begins to flow into our inboxes (though admittedly, I wouldn't be disappointed). The romantic overture of perfumed love letters arriving by snail mail will be a thing of the past, if they aren't already, but I foresee them being replaced by (oh no!) scented emoticons. Perhaps a rosy scent will accompany those popular pink and red hearts, zesty citrus scents will arrive with happy smiles and happy eyes, lilies for sorrow, musk for lust, rotting trash for anger or disgust. I cringe to imagine what might arrive should a relationship go on the rocks. One can only hope the sending and receiving of virtual scents through our devices will be optional, requiring perhaps the purchase of an app as opposed to an indiscriminate free flow of simulated smells into our inboxes.

An alternative to outdated perfumed love letters may be on the horizon. Like snapping a photograph, the capacity for replicating smell may one day include the ensnaring of body odour for commercial purposes. Such a remarkable advancement in scent technology would allow people like Laura, in chapter nine, to purchase a synthesized version of the scent of her beloved. London designer Amy Radcliffe is developing a specialized camera for capturing and recording an exact reproduction of aroma via an imaging system called The Madeleine. She uses techniques established by Swiss chemist Roman Kaiser in the 1970s for capturing smells for the fragrance industry. By holding a funnel (the nostril of this electronic nose) to an armpit, the odour particles are absorbed inside a resin trap. Once the captured scent is processed in a specialized lab, Radcliffe will transfer it into a tiny smell capsule, enclose it in a copper disk and deliver it to the purchaser.[68] Acquiring a scent portrait of a special person in their life would bring joy to many people. But synthetic fragrances aren't for everyone, and it's my guess Laura wouldn't choose to wear a locket containing an artificial replication of her lover's scent. She'd prefer the real deal.

Cyberscented Security

It's unlikely I'll be distributing *my* scent portrait to anyone anytime soon, and I plan to continue to be cautious regarding my personal security. I've resisted having my irises scanned for the sake of moving briskly through wait-lines at borders and airports. My irises are for my eyes only, thank you. Or so I thought. Full facial scanning—comparing a traveler's face with the image stored on his or her electronic passport—is already being implemented at airline check-in kiosks. And the technology for capturing body odour for an even more accurate identification solution may be arriving fast on its heels.[69]

The concept isn't original. Since the beginning of the twentieth century, odours have been collected at crime scenes and dogs have been brought in to match them with suspects in a police line-up. Today, "sniffer robots" decked out with electronic noses are programmed to be as equally adept as dogs for sniffing out human odours, drugs and other suspicious items at airports and borders, and one day our canine friends may find themselves unemployed.

However, in a development as seemingly futuristic as the Star Wars light sabres my sons played with as children, it's predicted a small rod will one day scan our skin for our scent profiles prior to being entered into a scent identification database. According to scent marketer C. Russell Brumfield, "a mere whiff of the essence of our skin will be one of the most radical changes to come in the new age of scent communication." [70]

World governments, law enforcement agencies, the military and financial institutions are on warp speed, researching and investing billions in high-tech odour identity systems. The tragedy of 9/11 gave governments the go-ahead to pull out all the stops when it comes to homeland security, and now smell banks hold the collected scent profiles of suspected terrorists, known criminals and miscellaneous samples taken from crime scenes. Lie detectors may one day become obsolete once e-noses are sufficiently refined to detect the spike in adrenaline that is an indicator of guilt for suspects under interrogation. The development of stench bombs for dispersing crowds is considered more efficient than tear gas in crowd control, and aerial spraying or detonating bombs containing odorous mind-altering chemicals have the potential to subdue aggressive armies and unsuspecting citizens into submission. Such lethal forms of manipulation are considered more humanitarian than the deployment of debilitating chemicals like "Agent Orange" used during the Vietnam War.

Google Gets in On the Action

The prospect of a future that includes mass mind control is highly controversial as well as troublesome, and it's difficult to foresee where the pursuance of such power could lead. On a lighter note, it's just as easy to be apprehensive about the smell of the future, knowing that corporations like Google are getting in on the scent revolution. Though most of my online life depends on Google's services, I'm suspicious of and often grumble about its all-seeing eyes. So, when I learned—through Googling of course—that the company had filed a patent for a digital deodorant, I was flummoxed. The new gadget, a wearable sensor, detects a rise in the wearer's activity that may result in sweating. When perspiration occurs, a fan emits a fragrance to cancel any forthcoming unpleasant odour.[71] Such a device might bolster the confidence of sweaty gym enthusiasts, cyclists or joggers on their circuits, but if the apparatus ever makes it to the marketplace, it's difficult to imagine it will be a bestseller. Successful or not, however, it's clear Google is nosing its way into the business of smell, determined not to be left behind.

Recently, through a little innocent eavesdropping, it didn't take me long to catch the drift of a conversation I overheard between two thirty-somethings in my local café. "I use it, I love it, I hate it," exclaimed one of them to his companion. The two were discussing the pros and cons of Google for connecting the citizens of the world. It's easy to empathize with their lamentations, though it might benefit them to drop their incessant habit of tilting their noses toward their devices and opt instead to tune in and turn on to nature. Doing so is especially essential to humanity's well-being as we plunge headlong into the future. Studies are showing that the internet and the Google-effect are changing our brains, altering our physiology, our memories, attention spans and sleep cycles, and changing how we think. In a phenomenon called neuroplasticity, it appears the brain begins to alter its behaviour based on new experiences, such as the tsunami of information presented by the internet and interactive technologies.[72]

Like an intoxicating perfume, the internet can snare one's attention. Paul Miller, a young American technology journalist who had been addicted to internet gaming, told his story to a TED Talk audience (a forum devoted to spreading ideas on technology, entertainment and design). He described the challenges he had experienced while attempting to give up his addiction by committing to an extended period of time away from any online activity. After a one-year sabbatical, he spoke of feeling "high," of wanting to see people more. He had space to think and time to be creative. And he confessed that "everything smelled better!" His sister told him he was also more emotionally available during this off-line period. But eventually, Paul became bored, began playing video games again, commenting that one can't be bored when always online. He admitted to feeling stressed with so much information coming in once again, and his sister said the wall between them was back up. [73]

I cite Paul's example because smell—so vitally connected with our survival instincts and basic needs—is also processed in the brain. Research has determined that as our brains become rewired, we begin to think, feel and even dream differently; subsequently, I question if a toxic overload of fragrance chemicals can potentially alter our brains. The odours of the natural world have accompanied and served humankind since our early ancestors practised incense burning rituals, but today scent diffusion systems of enormous capacity blast plumes of perfumed air into our indoor and outdoor environments. If synthetic aroma chemicals continue to compromise our innate sense of smell, implanted electronic noses could one day become a necessity.

The area of the neo-cortex in the logic-oriented left side of the brain represents eighty percent of the brain's function and that's already a huge chunk. Yet technology engineers are developing a synthetic extension of the neocortex, and it's predicted that within twenty years, our thinking could be both biological and non-biological. As technological progress drives humanity deeper into the realms of artificial intelligence and transhumanism, the prospect of synthetic brains and electronic noses in our future comes startlingly close to Huxley's concept of a brave new world.

It's my understanding the two sides of our brains were designed to serve us equally. The right side—the source of our basic instincts, motivation, emotional response, intuition and creativity—is where smell is processed. It is also where the qualities of love, compassion, caring, sharing, generosity and co-operation arise that define us as human beings. Considering humanity's present precarious state in its evolution, such qualities are required more urgently than ever. I am heartened by the circumspection of South African quantum physicist Neil Turok. At the conclusion of his book *The Universe Within*, he writes, "It is time to connect our science to our humanity and in doing so raise the sights of both. If we can only link our intelligence to our hearts, the doors are wide open to a brighter future." [74]

Weaning ourselves from artificial aromas and partaking fully in the fragrant opulence of nature will also contribute to a promising future. From the sublime to the quirky, plant aromatics regenerate the body and replenish the spirit. Even malodours serve a purpose. I vote for keeping my nose, my nostrils, my humanity.

Peppermint
Mentha piperita

Botanical Family:	*Lamiaceae*
Country of Origin:	England, France, Italy, USA
Fragrance Group:	Top note
Aroma:	Strong, fresh, green, minty herbal
Extraction Process:	Steam distillation
Derived From:	Fresh or partially dried herb
Valuable Uses:	Physical: antiseptic, anti-nausea, digestive issues, irritable bowel syndrome, headaches, aches and pains, bruising
	Mental/Emotional/Spiritual: shock, fatigue, mental fatigue; encourages concentration and increases vitality and vibrancy
Of Added interest:	Peppermint promotes calm as well as clarity as a result of the cooling and warming effect of its high menthol content.
Contraindications:	Avoid in pregnancy, when nursing and with children under three. Avoid with epileptics. May irritate sensitive skin. May antidote homeopathic remedies.

And the People Paused ...

*I*n March 2020, while most of us were looking the other way, the world changed irrevocably. The highly infectious Covid-19 virus, on the march out of Wuhan, China, was predicted to circle the globe, and people began stockpiling food, distancing and protecting themselves from each other and withdrawing into their homes. The elderly, ill and dying, isolated in hospitals and senior facilities, were denied the presence and comfort of loved ones. Yet during the early months of this period of fear and uncertainty, remarkable changes occurred. In being forced to slow down, people welcomed the stillness, contemplated life, started new projects and came to know each other and themselves more intimately. Motivated by concern for others, they checked in on, shopped for and took care of one another in a myriad of meaningful ways. Closing shopping malls reduced people's habitual spending and had the additional benefit of lessening their exposure to the pervasive presence of piped-in artificial aromas. And the decrease in air and automobile traffic created a significant reduction in pollution, facilitating cleaner air and easier breathing.

Scents that Comfort

Spring arrives early on Canada's West Coast. With more time on our hands than normal, we thronged to garden centres, spurred on by rumours of impending food shortages. While adjusting to the protocol of the pandemic, which called for physical distancing, we gauged our individual six-foot allotment of space as best we could, filled our trays and trolleys with plants and seedlings and lined up between the arrows at the check-out counters. Back in our gardens and down on our hands and knees, we planted flowers, potatoes, carrots and herbs. And as the fresh air and loamy soil penetrated our nostrils, filled our lungs and eased our anxiety, we were grateful for the diversion of gardening.

We also found comfort in our kitchens, and after stocking up on baking supplies, we dug out old recipe books, donned old aprons and filled our homes with scents of the sweet and the savoury— cookies, muffins, bread and cinnamon buns and labour-intensive dishes we'd always meant to try but hadn't dared to attempt in our hectic, pre-pandemic lives. The saying goes that when life gives you lemons, you make lemonade, and so a friend of mine—a gourmet cook living in Los Angeles who was down in the dumps due to recent lifestyle restrictions—initiated cooking classes on Zoom for family and friends. Inspired by the bounty of ripe lemons dangling from the trees, she kicked off her Sunday afternoon series with a recipe for a luscious lemon pound cake, which had us drooling over our kitchen counters and computers. And the following Sunday, pots of fragrant avgolemono soup—a Greek classic based on chicken and lemons—simmered on our stoves. In a similar creative vein—among the many options that filled our online viewing throughout the period of quarantine—I joined my friend Elaine on FaceTime to bake apple-rose pastries. The delicate little darlings rose to perfection and, when finished with a spritz of rosewater prior to serving, were worthy of high tea, as were the gluten-free apricot-citrus scones I had mastered the previous week.

Aromatic Health Strategies

Over and above the diversions of cooking and gardening for filling our time and supporting our psychological well-being, the top priorities on most people's agendas were to maintain good health and a sustainable income. As governments came to the financial aid of their citizens, Vitamin C disappeared from the shelves of health food stores, homeopathic pharmacies scrambled to keep up with the demand for flu-related remedies and essential oil companies enjoyed a brisk business in online sales. Everyone sought the elusive antidote to the Covid-19 virus.

In the weeks previous to the outbreak, I had been re-examining my research on the benefits of diffusing essential oils into areas such as medical settings where people congregate, and cross-contamination can be a concern. While doing so, I recalled my enthusiasm as a novice aromatherapist with a background in the health sciences on learning that exhaustive studies had proven the effectiveness of essential oils for inhibiting the growth of bacteria and viruses. At that time, in the 1990s, conventional medicine was skeptical of the benefits of scent molecules for decontaminating the air. But the overprescribing of antibiotics had resulted in antibiotic-resistant microorganisms, and it was my belief that essential oils were destined to become medicine's panacea for the future. Armed with my new knowledge, I went on to teach a class titled "Aromatherapy: Medicine for the Twenty-first Century." Now, twenty-five years later, the dilemma of the pandemic was presenting me with another opportunity for drawing attention to the powerful properties of aromatic plant remedies.

History informs us that perfumers and those working in herb and flower gardens had a higher resistance to the plagues that ran rampant throughout Europe in earlier centuries. In fact, in the early twentieth century, when French chemist René Gattefossé began studying the properties of essential oils, he encouraged hospital workers to use them for their protection during the Spanish flu epidemic. In *Advanced Aromatherapy,* chemist and pioneer of the science of aromatherapy Kurt Schnaubelt references the results of a 1955 Keller and Kober research project which disclosed that diffusing anti-infectious essential oils in an enclosed area not only controls airborne bacteria, it dramatically reduces or eliminates many infectious microorganisms.[75] Perhaps the climate of fear initiated by the pandemic crisis will alter the hesitancy of the allopathic medical community toward examining essential oils more closely as authentic anti-infectious agents and not simply pleasant-smelling mood enhancers.

The Tried and True

In Europe prior to the nineteenth century, it was common for people to carry pomanders and other forms of olfactory protection when they ventured out of doors. Medical doctors carried walking sticks with perfume boxes inserted in their tops that held aromatics with antiseptic properties. Before and after visiting contagious patients, they would pop open the box and inhale deeply. Some age-old traditions still in use throughout the world today employ plant essences as infection-reducing agents. For instance, friends of mine returning from Germany brought me a bottle of Melissengeist—spirit of melissa—a popular remedy and tonic in that country for nearly 200 years. Formulated in 1826 by Maria Clementine Martin, a German nun, the tonic is based on a soothing aromatic herb commonly known as lemon balm. The formula contains more than twenty essential oils, including melissa, clove, laurel, cinnamon, lavender, lemongrass, geranium and rose, and is meant to be taken internally. An in-depth study on the pharmacological effects of the primary components in this preparation has shown them to be effective against a host of microorganisms responsible for illnesses of the lungs and bronchial system.[76] Like Listerine mouthwash, formulated 150 years ago, Melissengeist is composed of essential oils steeped in alcohol and it's a powerfully strong and bracing tonic. My first sip not only took me by surprise, it nearly knocked me off my feet! To this day, the remedy continues to sit on the medicine shelves of many households in Germany and across Europe as an essential item for colds, flu and gastrointestinal issues. Unsurprisingly, there was a resurgence in sales with the onset of the pandemic.

Such is the case for a traditional remedy in Turkey. As in many countries in the early days of the Covid-19 outbreak, Turkey quickly ran out of commercial hand sanitizers, all of which are based on alcohol. Unlike in Canada, where distillers came to the rescue by producing hand sanitizers instead of rye, gin, whiskey and vodka, Turkey's minister of health stepped up the country's production of the aromatic *kolonya* or cologne. Since the days of the Ottoman Empire, which ruled much of the Middle East and the Mediterranean from the early fourteenth century to the twentieth century, kolonya has been a vital component of Turkish hospitality. Much more than an antiseptic, it is a familiar and beloved fragrance, and its formula contains the protective and mood-elevating essential oils of orange, bergamot, lemon and rosemary. Higher-end preparations also include jasmine, rose and fig blossoms. The formula, meant for external use only, symbolizes Turkey's deep-rooted custom of hospitality as well as its observance of good hygiene, and during the long periods of quarantine demanded by the pandemic, it evoked within Turkish citizens a sense of closeness and caring for one another. At the peak of the hand sanitizer shortfall, they stood in long lines in front of shops for many hours to stock up on kolonya—their "angel of mercy." On the other hand, Germany's Melissengeist could be considered the "little soldier." Though its primary ingredient, Melissa officinalis, is often called "the happiness herb," its taste is undeniably medicinal.

Treating viruses, including the Covid-19 strain, is more challenging than treating other forms of infection. Nevertheless, as in Germany and Turkey, my personal way of coping with the threatening pandemic was to put my trust in herbs and essential oils as a form of physiological protection and emotional support. And to be proactive, I made aromatherapy blends available to others in hopes of allaying some of their anxiety. The preparations included lavender, rosemary, lemon, cinnamon, clove, tea tree and thyme, essences extracted from plant materials commonly used in past centuries for their anti-infectious properties. When inhaling or applying these blends externally or diffusing them for purifying the air in my home, their warm, spicy aromas induced a feeling of comfort and well-being within me.

Research has shown that during times of heightened stress, remaining calm and maintaining a positive attitude and sense of being in control of one's life contributes to the optimal functioning and resiliency of the immune system. Therefore, as an adjunct to antiviral and anti-infectious remedies, I encouraged others to inhale calming, soothing aromas such as cedarwood, ylang ylang, lavender, neroli, rose and frankincense, essences that can be supportive to the nervous system.

Nature Nurtures

Though Covid-19 infection rates continued to fluctuate six months into the pandemic, air travel picked up once again. Many depended on it for work purposes, financial survival and miscellaneous commitments. Others began to abandon strict quarantine at home for an occasional getaway by car or for a nearby "staycation" or even a "daycation." Meanwhile, government health authorities proffered guidance for keeping infection rates under control, and mask-wearing became more prevalent, if not mandatory. Without a doubt, masks hamper our ability to fully flourish with our sense of smell, so I was in full agreement when health officials and practitioners encouraged us to get outdoors into the fresh air as frequently as possible. Exercising our bodies and aerating our lungs helps to elevate our mood. And allowing our noses and mouths freedom to carry out their normal and vital physiological functions without restriction is of critical importance to our overall well-being.

For my personal protection, I began a policy of carrying with me at all times a self-styled "Covid-19 protection pouch" complete with hand sanitizer, cotton masks and tiny bottles of essential oils. Whenever my breathing felt restricted or compromised while wearing a mask, I would add a drop or two of eucalyptus, spruce or frankincense to the centre of the mask for respiratory support. And at other times, when my spirits struggled to remain buoyant, I'd add an uplifting essence. Neroli, geranium and jasmine worked wonders on my mental and emotional constitution, and their antiseptic properties provided added protective benefits.

At Penn State University, on-campus students were expected to not only be part of a "Mask-Up or Pack-Up" regime but were also required to accept random testing for the virus. Periodically they received scratch-and-sniff cards, and if they experienced any sign of smell loss, they were required to self-isolate immediately and get tested. The good news was that this new Covid protocol included the placement of flower arrangements throughout the campus to encourage students to sniff and monitor their smell IQs. I like to imagine them lowering their masks momentarily to take long, deep restorative whiffs.

Taking Smell Seriously

The pandemic has been responsible for stirring up an enormous resurgence of interest in the sense of smell. In the early months of the outbreak, not only were frontline doctors losing their sense of smell, but others who had tested positive for the virus had experienced its sudden loss prior to the onset of the more common symptoms such as cough or fever. Sure enough, as the months passed, researchers determined that sixty percent of Covid-19 patients had an initial period of smell loss (anosmia), which resulted in the symptom being considered an important predictor of the illness. Not as widely reported was that victims of the virus also suffered from the loss of taste, since smell and taste are intimately linked.

In most cases, both senses returned quickly, for others, more slowly. However, for some people (dubbed "the long-haulers") it took up to six months for their full return—or they didn't return at all. Bereft of the sense of smell, people in these latter groups spoke of experiencing a feeling of disconnection, anger, anxiety and depression. They felt compelled to converse with others about their experiences and how they were feeling, which resulted in Facebook and other social media groups springing up worldwide.

Early research had determined it was the olfactory "support" cells that were infected, not the neurons that were responsible for detecting and transmitting the sense of smell to the brain. But to date, scientific research and theories surrounding the physiology of smell loss due to the Covid-19 viral infection remain inconclusive. Nevertheless, in a January 31, 2021 *New York Times* podcast titled *The Forgotten Sense*—which addresses the meaning of the strange symptom of the loss of smell associated with the virus—it was suggested that "Covid-19 arrived in a world that had spent far too long not taking the sense of smell seriously." [77]

Going Forward

Frontline workers have laboured tirelessly in antiseptic-laden corridors of clinics, hospitals and long-term care homes. In the early months of the lockdown, residents in my hometown paid them tribute every evening at seven PM, cheering, banging pots and clanging cymbals from their windows, decks and doors. I am saddened for those who have been adversely affected or who have lost loved ones and have been denied the opportunity to be present with them during their final moments. Though my personal experience throughout this daunting period of unprecedented change includes recollections of shock and uncertainty, I'm grateful it also includes positive and reassuring memories of aromas from my kitchen and garden, regenerating walks through the woods and healing remedies from my medicine kit.

Across the globe, families, friends, neighbours, strangers and those in conflict have had no other choice but to confront the unexpected challenges of a pandemic that has shifted our lives away from all that was comfortable and familiar. As lockdowns are avoided and the world returns to some semblance of order, we will gradually—though not always willingly—adjust to all that awaits us in the unfamiliar realm of the "new normal." Memories of this period in history—including scent memories both positive and negative—will remain with us for the rest of our lives and potentially be imprinted in our smell memory banks.

Humanity at the Crossroads

Prior to the pandemic, economists had been predicting the financial markets were due for a correction, yet in many ways it appeared humanity itself was due for a correction. Then, unexpectedly and without warning, we were awakened and reminded not only of our vulnerability as human beings, but of the fragility of life and the interdependency between all living things. I like to imagine that each person enters this world with a unique and valuable role for contributing to the betterment of the planet according their talents, abilities and capacity. The essence of that role lies deep within and deciphering its call often can't occur until we slow down long enough to listen.

The Covid-19 crisis has given us ample opportunity to be reflective. Throughout the world, growing numbers of people of every ethnicity, gender and age group, particularly Generation X and the Millennials, have aligned themselves with the growing trend in recent years to give up their high-tech, material-consumption lifestyles. Some have been prompted to return to the land to pursue regenerative agriculture and humane animal breeding, while others are growing and harvesting herbs, distilling essential oils, studying alternative medicine, promoting alternative energy systems and working for environmental organizations. This shift in ideology promises positive change for the future, and I have been impressed by the dedication and ongoing contributions of a number of these trailblazers:

✧ Master herbalist, aromatherapist and educator David Crow generously shares his expertise in the field of botanical medicine.

✧ Health activist Sayer Ji of GreenMedInfo and author of *Regenerate Yourself* promotes the concept of a "new biology" that challenges the present paradigm of germ theory.

✧ Internationally recognized educator and visionary Zach Bush MD seeks root-cause solutions for human and ecological health.

✧ Holistic psychiatrist Dr. Kelly Brogan practises drug-free psychiatry.

✧ Philosopher and author Charles Eisenstein inspires hope through his essays, talks and books, which include *The More Beautiful World Our Hearts Know Is Possible.*

Digging In

Food production and distribution have been disrupted by the ongoing challenges and uncertainty resulting from the pandemic and we're beginning to see the worldwide *Slow Food Movement* merging with the rapidly accelerating *Grow Food Revolution*. People are churning up their grassy lawns and transforming them into vegetable gardens, constructing raised beds on their patios and filling every available inch of their condo decks with pots for sprouting beans, potatoes, sweet peas and herbs. Rooftop gardens are flourishing in cities, and community gardens are popping up in vacant lots. We're flocking to local farmer's markets in record numbers, collecting and trading seeds, gathering up armfuls of lavender grown on nearby farms and purchasing organic vegetables, freshly laid eggs and fair-trade items that support growers in other parts of the world. One of my greatest pleasures is shopping at the roadside produce stands of local farms and returning home to prepare a fragrant and flavourful ratatouille or basil pesto, or roasting an organic chicken sprinkled with freshly snipped rosemary and thyme. Due to the pandemic, my nose is further attuned to the beneficence of the soil, and I give thanks daily for shelter, food on my table, and relatively stable weather conditions.

Heeding Nature

There is little certainty about anything any longer. In September 2020, my hometown was engulfed in throat-irritating smoke drifting north from wildfires raging out of control along the entire west coast of the U.S. As the inhalation of burnt ashes compromised our breathing, asthmatics, infants and the elderly were put at risks that surpassed the concerns of the pandemic. We lost the light and warmth of the sun and the freshness of the morning, while the aromatic grandeur of nature we tended to take for granted was temporarily suppressed.

In my part of the planet, most of us would never have imagined we'd be experiencing such dramatic effects of climate change. Yet to put it into perspective, 150 years ago no one could have predicted that one of the consequences of the rapid expansion of oil geysers that had dotted the plains of the North American landscape would be the development of the petrochemical industry that would go on to service two world wars, fuel and rule the economy and develop, dispense and rigorously promote a gamut of toxic chemicals across the globe. It also expanded to involve other industries that continue to this day to manufacture a preponderance of artificially scented products that are harmful to our bodies and the environment, tamper with our emotions and manipulate our spending. The lack of humanity's foresight has been calamitous.

People's knowledge regarding the dubious quality of ingredients that constitute cosmetic and body care products has increased significantly in recent decades, yet the simulated scenting of the air we breathe has burgeoned to extremes. Consumer awareness of this dilemma has been slower to catch on but hope glimmers on the horizon that this too is beginning to change.

Scientific exploration into the enigmatic and vastly untapped secrets of the sense of smell is expanding, and I expect it's only a matter of time before a second Nobel Prize is awarded to scientists in the field of olfaction. As the unfathomable value of smell, the neglected angel of the senses, garners greater recognition and asserts itself in the senses' hierarchy, we can only pray it will supersede any delusions about the dispensing of our noses or their replacement with electronic counterparts.

Rose Otto
Rosa damascena

Botanical Family:	*Rosaceae*
Country of Origin:	Bulgaria, Turkey, India, France
Fragrance Group:	Middle (heart) note
Aroma:	Rosy, lemony, fresh floral
Extraction Process:	Steam distillation
Derived From:	Fresh flower petals
Valuable Uses:	Physical: general tonic, anti-infectious, stimulant, improves circulation, female reproductive issues, infertility, childbirth aid, skin care
	Emotional/Mental/Spiritual: provides comfort during emotional crisis, heartbreak, grief, violated feelings; opens the heart
Of Added Interest:	Rose is considered the "Queen of Flowers." To preserve its aroma and protect its delicate petals from damage, the petals are picked before eight AM.
Contraindications:	None known

Flourishing with Our Sense of Smell

*A*merican poet Mary Oliver poses a startling question in her poem *One Summer Day*. "Tell me, what is it you plan to do with your one wild and precious life," she probes. But I think the question is not so much *what* you want to do with your life but *how* you want to do it and what influences will come to bear on it. The beginnings of my own journey were influenced by the fragrances in my father's bakeshop, but it was lavender's aromatic molecules looping across my 'smell-brain' like skywriting that clarified for me the answer to the poem's inquiry. And as I went on to explore the healing potential of olfaction, I became captivated by nature's wild and precious aromas.

Hanging out my shingle as an aromatic practitioner today would bring a far different response than it did twenty-five years ago. Not only is the sense of smell itself beginning to be acknowledged once again as a servant of our survival, but greater numbers of people are examining the health benefits of aromatic plant medicine. Essential oil sales have exploded into a 4.7-billion-dollar industry, and by 2022 these numbers are expected to increase by another twenty-two percent. North America's use represents about fifty-eight percent of world demand, followed by China and Japan.

The increased attention to the inherent value of the sense of smell is a positive turn. Forgetting or denying the odours of nature, of ourselves and of others not only severs our intuitive connection with the plant and animal worlds, but it separates us from our ancestral memories. Our forebears had rich olfactory lives unencumbered by the deodorants of modern life. They inhaled, harvested, supplemented their diets and supported their health with aromatic plants, and by integrating and savouring these same essential elements into our own lives, we carry their memories in our genes and forward them to succeeding generations. When we're out of touch with the natural world, we lose touch with ourselves, with our own essence, and thereby become more vulnerable to the influence of large corporations that demean our intelligence and our intuition while determining our habits. We allow them to dictate how we should look, what we should buy, how we should smell, and the pharmaceuticals we should ingest. "We're being manipulated into uniform mass consciousness," cautions essential oil researcher Kurt Schnaubelt.[78] I agree. And I believe it's time we turn up our noses at the amassing burden of artificial aroma that surrounds us, reclaim ownership of ourselves and our sense of smell, and become more aligned with the innate wisdom of our human nature.

Cultivating an Aromatic Life

Breathing keeps us alive, but smelling is fundamental to our well-being, and maintaining a conscious awareness of the odours that surround us can help us feel more fully alive. The good news is that it's never too late to train the brain to smell more acutely and discriminate between odours more accurately. In fact, with a little effort, anyone can exercise their right brain until mindful smelling becomes a habit. As a bonus, it's one form of fitness training that doesn't induce grumbling or procrastination. Therefore, I encourage everyone to become reacquainted, perhaps re-enchanted with their sense of smell and its life-sustaining benefits that accompany us throughout our lives from courtship to conception, through the teen years to the maturing years until the moment we take our final breath.

This final chapter offers a little olfactory coaching, and the routine is elementary. We simply need to smell ... smell ... smell

... as though our lives depended on it, since in many respects, the quality of our lives does indeed depend on it. Olfactory skills improve once greater attention is paid to the odours we normally take for granted, including those of our partners, our children, our coffee, toast, jam and toothpaste, the new day, a rainstorm, the interior of our car, the diversity of odours on public transportation and of our colleagues, offices and lunchrooms.

When immersed in an olfactory moment, try to follow these guidelines:

✧ Breathe deeply with intent.

✧ Be fully present and focus your attention on the smell in order to heighten your smell acuity.

✧ Be cognizant of the aromas that attract your attention and how they affect you. Are they comforting, repelling, enlivening, disturbing, and if so, why?

✧ What memories do certain odours evoke? How do they make you feel?

✧ Practise this new odour awareness on a daily basis. Keep a notebook for jotting down your impressions.

✧ Remember to take breaks. Olfactory fatigue can set in when an odour is smelled for an extended period of time.

After several weeks of focused sniffing, you may find yourself moving through life with your nose tilted upward and outward with a heightened curiosity about the world around you. In her book *Listening to Scent,* aromatherapist Jennifer Peace Rhind writes that working actively with the olfactory palette stimulates the senses and develops the part of the brain associated with the reasoning process.[79] I understand this to mean that both sides of the brain— the intuitive and the logical, can be balanced and coordinated. And as they begin to recharge, life will never *smell* the same.

Home Sweet Non-Toxic Home

Home is meant to be a haven—a refuge from the outer world— yet while attempting to create a pleasing environment, it's easy to unwittingly generate a hotbed of toxins. Many household cleaning supplies and heavy-duty detergents stored in cupboards and under sinks are comprised of harsh, perfumed, environment-destroying and immune-depleting chemicals that are not only hazardous but unnecessary. Detoxing our homes begins with a serious sweep through kitchens, bathrooms and laundry rooms, taking stock, scouring labels and discarding products with dubious ingredients. Baking soda, water, vinegar and a little elbow grease can replace most cleaning products, but since going back to basics isn't everyone's style, we are fortunate that numerous green-certified options are available for purchase.

An invaluable resource guide, *The Naturally Clean Home*, by Karyn Siegel-Maier, offers over 150 herbal/essential oil formulas for "green cleaning" every room, as well as recipes for dish and dishwasher blends, oven, furniture, floor and carpet cleaners, stain removers, laundry soaps, pot potpourri and sachets. Siegel-Maier's Tough Dirt and Grease Formula uses the grease-cutting, antibacterial power of vinegar for washing floors:

✧ 1 gallon of hot water

✧ 2 tablespoons of liquid castile soap such as Dr. Bronner's

✧ ¼ cup of washing soda

✧ 1 cup of vinegar

✧ 20 drops of eucalyptus, peppermint or tea tree essential oil

✧ Combine all of the above in a large bucket. Dip and mop using short strokes. No rinsing necessary. Voilà! An antiseptically clean floor without bleach!

Home Bacteria Busters

For decades, commercials have cautioned consumers against allowing unpleasant, telltale odours to linger in their homes as if the large conglomerates assume it's their moral duty to provide us with products that will magically eliminate such dreaded intruders. It's not surprising we've become habituated to camouflaging undesirable smells. Yet perhaps it's time we cultivated an acceptance of the common, everyday odours emitted from normal household routines, along with those of the people and pets who share our living spaces. I strongly recommend eliminating artificially scented air fresheners, sprays and plug-ins from every room. When necessary, we can bring in naturally scented alternatives that offer user-friendly, less toxic solutions, which not only freshen the air and defy bacteria, viruses, molds, but can give our mood a lift as well. For example:

✧ Diffusing eucalyptus, pine and spruce essential oils cleanses the air and provides respiratory and immune-boosting support.

✧ Lavender, lemon, lime, cinnamon, thyme, tea tree, clove and pine essential oils—diluted and blended or used singly—provide a highly effective anti-infectious solution for wiping down kitchen counters, sinks and toilets.

✧ Bergamot, orange, geranium and jasmine spritzed or diffused into a room enhances the ambiance during a social event and provides the added benefit of immune system protection.

Excluding synthetic scents from the home environment doesn't mean replacing them with an oversaturation of essential oils. Aromatherapy diffusers have become trendy, but more doesn't always mean better, and diffusers aren't meant to be run 24/7. Essential oils are concentrated plant medicines, 100-200 times stronger than their original plant sources, making caution and discretion in their use mandatory. It's preferable that diffusers be run for limited periods of time and for specific purposes, such as cleaning the air during and after there has been an illness in the home or for creating an amiable ambiance. And it's wise to remember that our olfactory biology deserves ample downtime in order to function effectively. A periodic "fragrance fast" to clear our bodily systems of chemical overload can be accomplished by eliminating all scented products from our homes and personal care regimes for one day a week or several days a month or longer. This allows our olfactory physiology as well as our bodies to rest, reset and become more finely tuned.

A Precious Commodity

Tons of raw plant material are required for the distillation of each essential oil. Yet, the yield of essential oil extracted from the distillation process amounts—on average—to only one percent of the total volume distilled. This leaves a staggering ninety-nine percent residual to be discarded or, at best, composted. Of added concern, many plants processed for the essential oil market are at risk of being overharvested. Some are already endangered. Therefore, it is prudent to research, make inquiries about and purchase essential oils from companies or stores whose suppliers have a reputation for employing sustainable, ethical practices. It is also recommended that essential oils be purchased in small quantities to prevent wastage. Such considerations serve the industry and the consumer as well as the environment.

The Aromatic Family

An aromatic birth is therapeutic for Mom and a beautiful way to welcome a new being into the world. Today, midwives at home-births and obstetrical nurses in progressive hospitals are employing essential oils throughout pregnancy and during labour, delivery and postpartum. They support a woman by enhancing a sense of well-being, alleviating anxiety and reducing discomfort and pain. For example:

✧ Two drops of ginger *or* peppermint essential oils blended with two drops of lemon essential oil and inhaled deeply when diffused in the air can alleviate morning sickness. Overall, diffuser time should be limited to no more than one hour in a twenty-four-hour time period.[80]

✧ Geranium is balancing and soothing in a backrub in the later stages of pregnancy.

✧ Rose acts as an antiseptic and uterine relaxant during labour.

✧ Neroli, diluted and spritzed in the labour room, is calming to the nervous system.

** It's best to avoid the application of essential oils on the skin during the first trimester of pregnancy. And it is highly recommended that a qualified essential oil professional be consulted prior to using essential oils during any stage of pregnancy.

Newborns arrive in the world with a highly sensitive olfactory acuity and are able to differentiate between the scent of their own mother and that of other mothers. While an infant is bonding with mom and adjusting to the profusion of odours in the environment, it's preferable that family members and visitors in the home or in the hospital be fragrance-free. In a baby's first year, gentle, high-quality herbal baby products may be all that is required for his or her care. For mothers wishing to use essential oils in the care of their babies, it's critical they be educated in the safe and effective use of these powerful essences. Clinical researcher and naturopath Dr. Jessie Hawkins believes there needs to be very good reasons to use essential oils on an infant under six months. For babies over six months as well as toddlers, she recommends starting with the gentle florals and milder citrus oils such as chamomile, lavender, mandarin and tangerine diluted in low concentrations (0.25–0.5 percent) in a carrier oil such as jojoba.

** It is imperative that all essential oils be stored in bottles with childproof caps and kept out of reach of children.

Often, older babies and toddlers will display signs of distress and separation anxiety when their mothers are absent for a period of time. Since a powerful bond is established between mother and child through the sense of smell, if Mom leaves a piece of her recently worn clothing behind, it can serve as a temporary substitute and help to console her child until her return.

Smells Like Daddy

Parents tend to direct their children's attention toward all that can be seen, heard, touched and tasted. They read them beautifully illustrated storybooks that include textures for touching, entertain them with whimsical CDs and rave enthusiastically about each spoonful of food they coax into their little one's mouth. But hang on a moment ... what about the sense of smell? Generally, smell is neglected in a child's early education. When my five-year-old granddaughter Charlotte stands on tiptoe, pokes a wildflower or a ripe peach under my nose and gushes, "Grandma, smell this," I know I'm doing my job. From the time she was able to sit, I wafted bananas, broccoli, rubber ducks, crayons, tiny vials of essential oils, even sour milk under her nose with the result that she has become conscious of the purpose of her nose and the smells that surround her. One day when she was exiting her family's condo, she found a hat lying on the stairway. She picked it up, took a good look, then a good whiff and blurted out to her mother, "It smells like Daddy!" As it turned out, Daddy had dropped his hat on the step on his way to work earlier that morning.

A sales clerk in an aromatherapy shop shared with me her unique approach to coping with her toddler's irrepressible urge to touch everything or put things in his mouth. She would divert his attention by suggesting he *smell* objects rather than touch them. I was impressed with her creative solution for encouraging her child to use his nose and not just his hands for exploring the enticing world of the senses, thereby bringing smell into his conscious awareness more readily. In my family, I've been assigned the role of "designated smell guide," and in making use of my title as a DSG, I offer the following suggestions for developing children's appreciation for their sense of smell:

✧ Bring to their attention and stimulate their appetites by discussing the aromas that fill the air when someone is cooking or baking.

✧ Stimulate their imagination and increase their vocabulary by having them describe what they're smelling. Since the sense of smell has a limited vocabulary, encourage children to be creative and make up new words for what they're smelling.

✧ Have children play smell-guessing games by blindfolding family members and friends, then running various foods and miscellaneous objects under their noses.

✧ While older children are eating and enjoying their food, have them pinch their nostrils closed, then ask them how their food tastes. This teaches them the connection between smell and taste, and they'll enjoy sharing this new trick with friends.

Infants tend to prefer sweet tastes and turn their heads away from strong vinegary or acidic smells, but overall, they come into the world neither liking nor disliking odours. In fact, babies and very young children aren't conscious of any great distinction between what adults consider good smells and bad smells. By the age of two or three, they may begin to differentiate between odours such as cookies baking in the oven and cabbage simmering on the stove. But many of our children's olfactory impressions come from the reactions of those around them, and a good example is when parents and caregivers scrunch up their noses—often playfully—and make negative comments while changing a diaper. A full diaper is the result of a normal biological process, so we should smile and celebrate! We can support children's awareness of their sense of smell from an early age by encouraging them to have an appreciation of all the smells in their indoor and outdoor environment. And it's helpful to explain that odours protect and warn as well as please; if some things don't smell good, it doesn't mean they're bad. Even rotting garbage and human waste are returned to the earth to complete a natural cycle.

Family Smell Therapy

Being out in nature is revitalizing and can make people feel like their best selves. So, whether alone or with family or friends, consider making smell strolls part of your outdoor routine. Have fellow strollers share their stories and experiences about their sense of smell. Encourage them to communicate their impressions about the odours they detect along the route—such as the sweet, heady aroma wafting from a bush of wild roses, fresh muffins and coffee beckoning from a local café, fragrant planks of cedarwood at a building site, or the smell of gasoline and oil at a corner service station.

During a walk through the woods or a forest, the aroma of pine needles crushed underfoot can unconsciously deepen the breath, loosen tight shoulders and quiet a chattering mind. The noise in cities taxes the brain in its attempt to filter out the cacophony, but the brain relaxes in nature where it isn't required to work as hard.

179

This theory is supported by American journalist Richard Louv in his *New York Times* bestseller, *Last Child in the Woods: Saving our Children from Nature-Deficit Disorder.* He suggests the increasing incidence of attention disorder in large cities throughout the world decreases when children are immersed in nature. With this in mind, it's no surprise that "forest bathing" has grown in popularity throughout the world as a trendy, wellness-boosting pastime. The Japanese Ministry of Agriculture, Forestry and Fisheries coined the term in 1982 and recommended it as part of its public health program. Citizens were advised to take time away from their hectic lifestyles to bathe in the healing power of nature.

The fragrant oils released from the bark, wood, leaves, needles and resins of a variety of trees, including pine, fir, spruce, cedarwood and cypress, contribute to the calming, almost sacred atmosphere of a forest. In the extraordinary documentary *Call of the Forest: The Forgotten Wisdom of Trees,* released in 2016, classical botanist Diana Beresford-Kroeger describes the forest experience as "immersing yourself in the bath of medicinal aerosols that make up the forest atmosphere." [81] Though the chemical makeup of these essences—or aerosols, as Beresford-Kroeger terms them—acts as a defence mechanism for the trees, they serve our human biology as well. Inhaling them as we meander through the woods stimulates the release of neurotransmitters and hormones that lower blood pressure, pulse rate and blood cortisol levels that rise when we're stressed. We begin to feel more grounded, invigorated, refreshed. As a bonus, the antiseptic, antibacterial and antiviral properties dispersed into the air by these medicinal aerosols bolster our immune systems.

Time spent in the woods is not only refreshing and immune-boosting but also free, easy and pleasurable to enjoy alone or in the company of others. And as an all-seasons activity that benefits young and old, it's also reputed to promote harmony in relationships. Such benefits appear to be sufficient reason for getting our families out of the malls, away from their screens and into the woods for a day of tree-hugging now and then. And when nasty weather or a busy schedule deter us from communing with nature, we can bring the outdoors in by inhaling a few drops of black spruce or cedarwood essential oil from a tissue, diffusing a room with a blend of coniferous essential oils, or adding several drops to a log in the fireplace before lighting. With very little effort, the overburdened neurons in the brain are refreshed, the chattering of the mind diminishes, and the body begins to relax.

Dirt's In!

Aside from exceptional circumstances such as the Covid-19 pandemic, western society's obsession with cleanliness and overuse of antibiotics and scented hand sanitizers strips away the good bugs along with the bad, leaving our immune systems more vulnerable than ever. Furthermore, the medical community's recent "hygiene hypothesis" suggests that too much cleanliness may contribute to children as well as adults developing allergies, asthma, inflammatory bowel diseases, and other autoimmune disorders. Soil-based organisms, including those released from nutrient-rich forest floors, support our immunity. So, when planting pots, window boxes, private or community gardens, encourage family members to plow their hands into the rich, musty earth and inhale heartily.

For her PhD degree in Environmental Design and Planning, my friend Illène Pevec, a resident of Colorado, did her doctoral research on youth involved in school and community gardening programs. Her objective was to learn what impact gardening had on their emotional, mental and physical well-being, and her resulting book, *Growing a Life: Teen Gardeners Harvest Food, Health and Joy,* is a testament to the benefits of community gardening programs for teens. High school students from a cross-section of ethnicities born in the US and abroad reported on the feelings of peace and calm they experienced while gardening and inhaling the aromas of a variety of plants and herbs such as lavender, mint and the piquant scent of tomato plants. The teens relished being outdoors in the fresh air as opposed to indoors in stuffy classrooms. When discussing roses, Marcella from Colorado said, "Really nice smells relax me." And Rosemary from Alaska wrote:

I've never had a bad time gardening.

That smell puts me

In the zone of calm,

Cool and collected.

Nurturing Our Teens

As teenagers struggle for independence, they continue to need touch and affection to support them in feeling accepted and comfortable in their bodies. The French word "sentir" means to feel, to touch, and I was delighted to learn it also means to smell. Since both smell and touch are processed in the limbic system that governs the right side of the brain, they complement each other, and I used this powerful pairing of the senses to heighten my connection with my eldest granddaughter. Though distance prevented Maren and me from seeing each other frequently, during every visit until she was into her late teens, I offered her a lavender-scented foot or back massage, which she accepted without fail. If on occasion I'd forget, she'd remind me. Through the senses, we fostered a loving connection, which I hope will be incorporated into her own parenting one day.

While adjusting to the developmental changes that are part of the growth process, including sexual awareness, teens may benefit when introduced to a balanced health care plan. It can begin with an appointment with a medical professional they trust and feel comfortable with, such as a family doctor. Parents can also encourage and assist their teens in consulting a complementary health practitioner, perhaps a naturopath, homeopath, herbalist, aromatherapist or massage therapist. Doing so will introduce them to the many benefits of alternative approaches to health care that are available as well as to natural-based products. One of my aromatherapy massage clients occasionally booked massages for her teenage daughters. During my sessions with them, I observed that their ability to relax and the comfort level they had with their bodies could likely be attributed to their awareness of how much their mother, a single parent, benefited from having regular massages. Our teenagers are our future. As such, they deserve to be heard, understood, guided and educated on the value of self-awareness and self-care, which includes the nurturing of their minds, bodies, emotions, spirits and all of their senses.

The Mating Game

The introduction of "the pill" in the 1960s transformed the dynamics of our society, and the popular slogan "make love, not war" was particularly influential. Not missing a beat, the baby boom generation took the slogan to heart and used it to its full advantage. The pill—comprised of synthetic steroid hormones—allowed women to be sexually active within or without marriage without the fear of pregnancy. Now, fifty years later, the pill is coming under scrutiny. Millions of women are speaking up about their struggle with a diverse variety of complaints in what has recently been labelled "post birth control syndrome." The symptomatology includes infertility, difficulty conceiving, difficulty returning to normal menstrual patterns, headaches, hair loss, low libido and chronic yeast infections. And the rates of hormone-related symptoms, such as mood swings, anxiety and depression, are climbing.[82]

As a result, many women are turning to non-hormonal forms of birth control, including IUD's, diaphragms and fertility tracking. This movement toward a more natural approach to contraception may prove to be an important trend in light of the recent research that hormonal contraception alters a woman's sense of smell and could thereby influence her choice of a mate. The quandary is how to use this information. Some health professionals are recommending that women allow their bodies to choose the right partner without the hormonal interference induced by pills. In the meantime, non-hormonal contraceptives can be used as an alternative. At the very least, physicians could be more proactive about informing women of the potential side effects of hormonal steroids while science continues to investigate their influence on relationships and mate selection.

Savouring Scent

If women spent as much time sniffing out the right mate as experienced cooks spend sniffing out the right ingredients, we could very well produce a new generation of gourmet babies. The *Slow Food Movement* began in Rome in 1986 for the purpose of resisting the opening of a McDonald's near the Spanish Steps. With now over 100,000 members in 160 countries, this campaign recommends that people slow down, savour and celebrate food, flavour, aroma, taste, culture and tradition, while it opposes fast food, industrial food production and globalization. To this sage advice, I offer a few tips related to olfaction for the modern family to consider:

✧ Slowing down and cooking for pleasure with children, partners, friends and family makes for a happy household.

✧ Inhaling deeply through the nose over one's food prior to eating connects the odour molecules from food with the satiety centre of the brain, making us more conscious of when we're full.

✧ Fast foods are less satisfying. They tend to be bland and are rarely highly odorous unless they've been plugged with artificial flavours and scents.

✧ Eating mindlessly in front of TVs or computers diverts attention away from the food and leads to a decrease in taste and satiety levels. We tend to eat more when we're less satisfied.

✧ Sniffing herbs, spices and condiments as they're being added to a pot or serving dish while discussing with others their culinary purpose, makes cooking an educational adventure.

✧ Sampling food as the flavours develop enhances the adventure.

Bringing essential oils and floral waters into cooking and baking adds a creative touch as well as an olfactory flavour boost. For instance, the addition of a teaspoon of rosewater can transform a summer fruit salad into a fruity-floral extravaganza. Several drops of zesty lemon essential oil will rescue a hollandaise sauce when lemons were missed on the shopping list. A scant drop of lavender added to whipped cream and topped with a sprinkle of lavender petals will add visual as well as fragrance and taste appeal to cakes, cookies, scones and squares.

Smell Loss Training

When the sense of smell diminishes or is lost, the joy of cooking and other pleasures of life are diminished along with it. Whether the loss is due to such disorders as a respiratory infection or head trauma, doctors often feel helpless in proposing treatment. Fortunately, smell clinics are popping up across the globe and patients afflicted with olfactory dysfunction are being offered smell training. The protocol often consists of repeated, short-term exposure over a period of time to high-intensity odours, such as lemon, eucalyptus, rose and clove essential oils. Smell training is in its early stages of development and to date, it appears the chances of recovery depend on the severity of the damage.

Aging Well with Your Sense of Smell

The nonprofit organization Fifth Sense, based in the UK, offers online support for people suffering from smell and taste disorders. Its website reports that at least a quarter of those over fifty-five years and nearly two-thirds of those over eighty years have a diminished sense of smell. Yet unlike vision or hearing loss—which is often apparent to others before the afflicted person themselves—a loss of smell and taste sensitivity occurs gradually and can go undetected. Early signs may be a diminished interest in food, gradual weight loss, or a tendency to over-season foods with salt and sugar. There may even be audacious complaints like those of my aging father, who, in his late nineties, began insisting that the food served at the long-term care home where he resided was tasteless and contained cardboard.

However, today's middle-agers and baby boomers are determined *not* to age. And since they like to remain current on all the trends for staying healthy and fit, I say it's high time *olfactory* fitness is included in the equation. Educating oneself about the aromas that enhance concentration, focus, memory, mood and food and the overall enjoyment of life can serve as a valuable supplement to the aging journey. For example:

◈ Inhaling favourite scents can boost one's spirits.

◈ Rosemary essential oil, when inhaled, focuses the mind. When ingested in the form of an herbal tincture, it acts as a general tonic.

◈ Chamomile, marjoram and valerian herbs and essential oils promote sleep.

◈ Geranium essential oil diluted and massaged into the feet, legs, hands and arms aids circulation and is a mood enhancer.

◈ Lavender, neroli and ylang ylang essential oils are calming, reduce anxiety, and are especially beneficial in baths and foot-baths. I can never heap enough praise upon lavender, and any discussion on well-being in aging wouldn't be complete without it. Multiple studies have revealed results for lavender's remarkable capacity for improving sleep, relieving pain and reducing stress by lowering blood pressure, heart rate and skin temperature.

** Caution in the use of lavender is recommended for anyone with very low blood pressure.

It's advised that commercial perfumes and scented products be used sparingly by aging adults. The sense of smell slowly diminishes with age, and it's common for seniors to be unaware they are overdoing the application of these products. Doing so may suit them, but it is not always appreciated by those in their vicinity. It's also good to remember that seniors require fresh, nourishing foods. The meals served in many care facilities are mass-produced, overcooked and tasteless. Family and friends can bring in appealing foods enhanced with aromatic herbs, spices, essential oils and condiments.

The Dementia Dilemma

According to neurologist Dr. David Perlmutter, there are no pharmaceutical approaches to date that have any meaningful effectiveness in the treatment of Alzheimer's. On his website, he cites a 2018 report from the *Neurology* journal indicating that the five marketed medications for the condition offer limited benefits for a limited number of patients. Though the pharmaceutical industry's failure to formulate an effective medication is frustrating and disappointing, researchers are learning that physical exercise, remaining socially engaged and keeping the brain active with ongoing learning can slow the progression of the disease. Studies also support the use of aromatherapy as a non-pharmacological treatment for symptoms of the condition, such as anxiety, confusion and irritability. For example:

✧ Rosemary essential oil diluted and applied topically or inhaled in the morning can heighten concentration, cognitive function and relieve depression.

✧ Lavender, chamomile and orange are a calming synergy for the evening. The application of these gentle oils in a soothing hand and foot massage can be beneficial for decreasing aggression, anxiety and for improving sleep.

✧ Sipping lavender or chamomile tea can be calming to the nervous system.

None of us know what the future holds, but we do know that smell, like music, is inextricably linked with memory and with the past. A 2002 study at the University of Warwick, England, revealed that offering meaningful olfactory cues to the aged while verbally reminiscing about the autobiographical memories associated with these aromas can assist in the retrieval of long-forgotten memories.[83] With this in mind, I encourage everyone to advise friends and family of the scents that have been meaningful to them throughout their lives, along with a description of the situations and experiences which made them meaningful. Filing a memorandum of scent memories alongside other important papers, medical instructions, last wishes and wills, becomes an invaluable tool of communication in one's later years.

A Fragrant Transition

From my experiences at the bedside of my dying parents and others with whom I have been close in my life, I have become immensely appreciative of the services offered by palliative and hospice care, whether at home or in a hospital. The objective of these services is to improve the quality of life for those who are suffering a life-ending illness. Ideally, the patient is moved to a peaceful setting separate from the frantic pace and antiseptic odours of hospital wards. Normally, all treatment and medication are discontinued, and pain management is readily available. The primary purpose of care is to maintain the person's comfort while supporting his or her emotional and spiritual needs.

With the permission of hospital staff, the family and, when applicable, the person themselves, spritzing a low concentration of rose or neroli essential oil, or administering them in a foot or hand massage, can soothe and comfort, relieve anxiety and assist the patient in their transition. The lingering scents may also offer solace to caregivers and family members at the patient's bedside as another soul's journey in the circle of life arrives at its final conclusion.

Pilgrims on the Fragrant Path

Decades have whirled by since my nose led me down the aisles of my father's bakeshop, lured me into the perfume salons of Paris and ushered me into "smell school." My ardour for nature's beautiful, health-enhancing aromas has motivated me to share with others not only the mysteries that encompass the invisible universe at the tip of our noses but to implore that we be mindful and cautious of all that we inhale through our nostrils and thereby our bodies, our minds and our spirits.

I recall with fondness the cautioning of my early teachers that immersing oneself in the world of aromas could lead to a harmless form of addiction. It appears their warnings were prophetic since many of my former instructors, classmates and colleagues remain active in the field today. I am grateful for the teachers and mentors who have influenced my fragrant calling, as well as the growers, distillers and producers of raw aromatic materials who labour in small and large farms in developing countries across the globe. Currently, a new generation of distillers are striving to establish essential oil production in North America, and several lavender fields are flourishing in my hometown on British Columbia's Sunshine Coast.

As a passionate advocate for the sense of smell, I hope this book will serve as a reminder of its crucial and irreplaceable role in our survival. Being human and fully alive with all of our senses intact is a privilege. May we individually and collectively hang on to that privilege—for dear life.

When peaceful cities are blessed with myriad sweet floral scents; when healthy forests are filled with balsamic coniferous perfumes; when farms are enveloped in the earthy aromas of healthy soil and robust crops; when homes are infused with temple essences that bring joy and tranquility, we will understand why the ancients taught that plants were gifts from heaven.

The Alchemy of Fragrance, David Crow

Endnotes

Part One

1–8 The Mystery of Smell

1   Piesse, G.W. Septimus. "The Art of Perfumery." Philadelphia: Lindsay and Blakiston, 1867. Website: https://www.gutenberg.org/files/16378/16378-h/16378-h.htm

2   Bomback, Andrew, M.D. (2006, January 2). *The Physical Exam and the Sense of Smell*, New England Journal of Medicine. Retrieved from http://www.nejm.org/doi/full/10.1056/NEJMp048244

3   Porter...Noam Sobel. (2006, December 17). *Mechanisms of Scent-tracking in Humans.* Nature Neuroscience. Retrieved from https://www.nature.com/articles/nn1819
    https://www.ncbi.nlm.nih.gov/pubmed/17173046
    https://www.washingtonpost.com/news/morning-mix/wp/2015/10/23/scottish-woman-detects-a-musky-smell-that-could-radically-improve-how-parkinsons-disease-is-diagnosed/

4   Quigley. (2015, October 21). "The Woman Who Can Smell Parkinson's Disease." Website: https://www.bbc.com/news/uk-scotland-34583642

5   Bindel. (2015, April 27). "I Lost My Sense of Smell-It Was Hard Not to Panic." Website: https://www.theguardian.com/commentisfree/2015/apr/27/lost-sense-of-smell-perfume-flowers-smoke-coffee

6   The Economist. (2014, October 14). "The Scent of Death." Website: https://www.economist.com/science-and-technology/2014/10/02/the-scent-of-death

7   Brillat-Savarin J.A. *The Physiology of Taste*. London: Penguin Books: 1825. 1994.

8   American Physiological Society. (2018, July 12). "Smell Receptors in the Body Could Help Sniff Out Disease." Website: https://www.sciencedaily.com/releases/2018/07/180712100214.htm

9–10　Initiation into Smell School

9　Piesse, G.W. Septimus. (1867). *The Art of Perfumery*. Philadelphia: Lindsay and Blakiston. Website: https://www.gutenberg.org/files/16378/16378-h/16378-h.htm

10　Schnaubelt, Kurt. *Medical Aromatherapy*. Berkeley: Frog Books, 1999, p. 125.

11–13　Loss of Aromatics as Remedies

11　Alain Corbin. *The Foul and the Fragrant*. Cambridge, MA: Harvard University Press, 1986, p. 56.

12　Gattefossé, René Maurice. *Gattefossé's Aromatherapy*, Saffron Walden UK: C.W. Daniel Company Limited, 1993.

13　Ryman. "Maury." Website: http://danieleryman.com/portfolio/marguerite-maury/

14–16　Fragrant Grace

14　Hypotheses. (2013, October 10). "Female Perfume Makers in Neo-Assyrian and Babylonian Documents." Website: https://refema.hypotheses.org/806#_ftn1

15　Ashbrook Harvey. *Scenting Salvation*. Oakland, CA. University of California Press, p. 22.

16　YouTube. The Coronation of Queen Elizabeth 11. "The Holy Anointing. "Website: https://www.youtube.com/watch?v=ZYay408Rd7c

17–18　The Golden Age of Perfumery

17　Rovesti, Paolo. *In Search of Perfumes Lost*. Venice: Blow-up, 1980, p. 9.

18　Aftel, Mandy. *Essence and Alchemy*. New York: North Point Press, 2001, p. 9.

Part Two

19-23　Subliminal Persuasion

19　Firstenberg, Arthur. *The Invisible Rainbow*. Chelsea Green Publishing, 2020, p. 134.

20　Brumfield, C. Russell. *Whiff*. New York: First Quimby Press, 2008. P. 12.

21 Suskind, Patrick. *Perfume*. London: Penguin Books, 1987, p. 161.

22 Huxley, Aldous. *Brave New World Revisited*. Harper & Brothers, 1958.

23 ibid., 309.

24–28 The Perils of Perfume

24 sixwise.com. "The Toxic Danger of Fabric Softener and Dryer Sheets." Website: http://www.sixwise.com/newsletters/05/02/08/the_toxic_danger_of_fabric_softener_and_dryer_sheets.htm

25 David Suzuki Foundation. (2011, June). "Failing the Sniff Test." Website: https://davidsuzuki.org/wp-content/uploads/2011/06/failing-sniff-test-chemicals-fragranced-personal-care-products.pdf

26 Environmental Working Group. (2007, February 8). "EWG Research Shows 22 Percent of All Cosmetics May be Contaminated with Cancer-Causing Impurity." Website: https://www.ewg.org/news/news-releases/2007/02/08/ewg-research-shows-22-percent-all-cosmetics-may-be-contaminated-cancer#.W3R9UC0ZMxc

27 Byatt, A.S. (2001, September 1). "How We Lost Our Sense of Smell." Website: https://www.theguardian.com/books/2001/sep/01/scienceandnature.asbyatt

28 Worwood, Valerie Ann. *The Fragrant Mind*. London: Doubleday, 1995, p. 57.

Part Two

29–41 Triggers of the Psyche

29 CBC Radio. (2017, February 2). "You Can't Look Away from a Smell." Website: https://www.cbc.ca/radio/thecurrent/the-current-for-february-2-2017-1.3962070/you-can-t-look-away-from-a-smell-a-reporter-s-struggle-with-ptsd-1.3962105

30 Randerson. (2008, December 3). "The Smell of Fear is Real Say Scientists." Website: https://www.theguardian.com/science/2008/dec/03/fear-smell-pheromone

31 NCBI. "The Scent of Fear." Website: https://www.ncbi.nlm.nih.gov/pubmed/12011790

32 Randerson. (2008, December 3). "The Smell of Fear is Real Say Scientists." Website: https://www.theguardian.com/science/2008/dec/03/fear-smell-pheromone

33 Classen, Constance, David Howes and Anthony Synnott. *Aroma.* London: Routledge, 1994, p. 196.

34 YouTube. (2017, April 15). "Does Canadian Money Really Smell Like Maple Syrup?" Website: https://www.youtube.com/watch?v=2KEQCudRqbY

35 Association for Psychological Science. (2015, April 16). "A Sniff of Happiness." Website: https://www.psychologicalscience.org/news/releases/a-sniff-of-happiness-chemicals-in-sweat-may-convey-positive-emotion.html

36 Coghlan. (2010, November 3). "Genes Marked by Stress Make Grandchildren Mentally Ill." Website: https://www.newscientist.com/article/mg20827853-500-genes-marked-by-stress-make-grandchildren-mentally-ill/

37 NCBI. (2017, April 25). "Secondary Traumatic Stress in Spouses of Veterans with PTSD." Website: https://www.ncbi.nlm.nih.gov/pmc/articles/PMC5459293/

38 Horsthemke. (2018, July 30). "A Critical View on Transgenerational Epigenetic Inheritance in Humans." Website: https://www.nature.com/articles/s41467-018-05445-5

39 Gilbert, Avery. *What the Nose Knows*. New York: Crown Publishers, 2008, p. 60.

40 Hertz, Rachel PhD. *The Lure of Aromatherapy*. Nutritional Health Review, Vol. 102, 2010.

41 Schnaubelt, Kurt. *Medical Aromatherapy*. Berkeley: Frog Books, 1999, p. 19.

42-63 Love, Lust and Body Odour

42 Le Guérer, Annick. *Scent*. New York: Random House, 1992, p. 197.

43 ibid., 218.

44 Rumi, Jalāl ad-Dīn Muhammad Rūmī. *Rumi's Little Book of Life*. Newburyport, MA: Hampton Roads Publishing, 2012.

45 Devlin. (2015, March3). Palm-scent: "The Science of Smelling After a Handshake." Website: https://

www.theguardian.com/science/2015/mar/03/
palm-scent-the-science-of-smelling-after-a-handshake

46 Environmental Working Group. "Top Tips for Safer Products."
    Website: https://www.ewg.org/skindeep/top-tips-for-safer-products/

47 Artemis. *Renegade Beauty.* Berkeley, CA: North Atlantic Books, 2017,
    p. 5.

48 Le Guérer, Annick. *Scent.* New York, Turtle Bay Books, p. 10.

49 Bryant. (1996, March 1). "The Smell of Love." Website:
    https://www.psychologytoday.com/ca/articles/199603/
    the-smell-love

50 Worwood, Valerie Ann. *Aromantics.* Great Britain: Pan Books, 1987,
    p. 17.

51 Skloot. (2007, December 9). "Lap-Dance Science." Website:
    https://www.nytimes.com/2007/12/09/magazine/09lapdance.html

52 Classen, Constance, David Howes and Anthony Synnott. *Aroma.*
    London: Routledge, 1994, p. 91.

53 Aftel, Mandy. *Essence and Alchemy.* New York: North Point Press,
    2001, p. 88.

54 Reuter Health. (2007, January 21.) "Viagra May Decrease
    Ability to Smell." Website: https://www.reuters.com/article/
    us-viagra-smell-idUSKNE78551720070117

55 Dalrymple, William. *Scents and Sensuality.* The Economist, January 4,
    2017.

56 Worwood, Valerie Ann. *Aromantics.* London: Bantam Books, 1993,
    p. 24.

57 Hale, Sharon. *Book of a Thousand Days.* London: Bloomsbury
    Publishing, p. 149.

58 NCBI. "Sexual Dimorphism in Human Olfactory Bulb." Website:
    https://www.ncbi.nlm.nih.gov/pmc/articles/PMC4221136/

59 NCBI. (2014, August 5). "Sexual Attractiveness in Male Chemicals
    and Vocalizations in Mice." Website: https://www.ncbi.nlm.nih.
    gov/pmc/articles/PMC4122165/

60 Royal Society. (2011, October 12). "Relationship Satisfaction and
    Outcome in Women who Meet Their Partner While Using Oral
    Contraception." Website: https://royalsocietypublishing.org/doi/
    full/10.1098/rspb.2011.1647

61   Wenner. (2008, December 1). "Birth Control Pills Affect Women's Taste in Men." Website: https://www.scientificamerican.com/article/birth-control-pills-affect-womens-taste/

62   PMC. (2008, August 12). "MHC-correlated Odour Preferences in Humans and the Use of Oral Contraceptives." Website: https://www.ncbi.nlm.nih.gov/pmc/articles/PMC2605820/

63   The Royal Society. (2011, October 12). "Relationship Satisfaction and Outcome in Women Who Meet Their Partner While Using Oral Contraception." Website: https://royalsocietypublishing.org/doi/full/10.1098/rspb.2011.1647

Part Three

64-74   The Fragrant Future

64   Poster. Selected Writings. Jean Baudrillard. "Simulacra and Simulation." Website: https://web.stanford.edu/class/history34q/readings/Baudrillard/Baudrillard_Simulacra.html

65   Classen, Constance, David Howes and Anthony Synnott. *Aroma*. London: Routledge, 1994, p. 200.

66   Avery, Gilbert. *What the Nose Knows*. New York: Crown Publishing, 2008, p. 149.

67   ibid., 147

68   Calouro. (2013, June 28). "Scent-ography." Website: https://petapixel.com/2013/06/28/scent-ography-this-camera-captures-smells-instead-of-pictures/

69   Science Daily. (2014, February 4). "Identity Verification: Body Odour as a Biometric Identifier." Website: https://www.sciencedaily.com/releases/2014/02/140204073823.htm

70   Brumfield, C. Russell. *Whiff*. New York: First Quimby Press, 2008, p. 23.

71   Murphy. (2015, February 14). "Google Gets Patent for Body Odour-Sensing Device." Website: https://www.pcmag.com/news/google-gets-patent-for-body-odor-sensing-device

72   Hiscott. (2014, March 14). "Eight Ways Tech Has Completely Rewired Our Brains." Website: https://mashable.com/2014/03/14/tech-brains-neuroplasticity/

73 TEDx. (2013, September 13). "A Year Offline and What I Have Learned." Website: https://www.youtube.com/watch?v=trVzyG4zFMU

74 Turok, Neil. *The Universe Within*. Toronto: Anansi Press, 2012, p. 257.

75-78 And the People Paused …

75 Schnaubelt, Kurt. *Advanced Aromatherapy*. Vermont: Healing Arts Press, 1998, p. 31.

76 ibid., 33.

77 New York Times. (2021, January 21). Podcast. "The Forgotten Sense". Website: https://www.nytimes.com/2021/01/31/podcasts/the-daily/coronavirus-loss-of-smell-anosmia.html

78 Schnaubelt, Kurt. *Medical Aromatherapy*. Berkeley: Frog Books, 1999, p. 23.

78-83 Flourishing with Our Sense of Smell

79 Rhind, Jennifer Peace. *Listening to Scent*. London: Singing Dragon, 2014, p. 22.

80 Tisserand Aromatherapy. "Essential Oils During Conception, Pregnancy and Beyond. Website: https://www.tisserand.com/blog/aromatherapy/how-to-use-essential-oils-during-conception-pregnancy-and-beyond/

81 Treespeak Films. "Call of the Forest." Website: http://calloftheforest.ca

82 Brighten. (2013, February 6). "Post-Birth Control Syndrome and How to Heal Now." Website: https://drbrighten.com/post-birth-control-syndrome/

83. PubMed. "Preserved Olfactory Cuing of Autobiographical Memories in Old Age." Website: from https://www.ncbi.nlm.nih.gov/m/pubmed/11773222/

Bibliography

Ackerman, Diane. *A Natural History of the Senses*. New York: Vintage, 1990.

Aftel, Mandy. *Essence and Alchemy*. New York: North Point Press, 2001.

Aftel, Mandy. *Fragrant*. New York: Riverhead Books, 2014.

Arctander, Steffen. *Perfume and Flavour Materials of Natural Origin*. Illinois: Allured Publishing, 2003.

Ashbrook Harvey, Susan. *Scenting Salvation*. Oakland, CA: University of California Press, 2006.

Artemis, Nadine. *Renegade Beauty*. Berkeley: North Atlantic Books, 2017.

Avery, Gilbert. *What the Nose Knows*. New York: Crown Publishing, 2008.

Beauieu, Denyse. *The Perfume Lover*. Toronto: Penguin Group, 2012.

Brogan, Kelly, M.D. *Own Yourself*. Hay House, 2019.

Buhner, Stephen Harrod. *The Healing Power of Plants*. New York: Simon and Schuster, 2012.

Burr, Chandler. *The Emperor of Scent*. New York: Random House, 2004.

Brumfield, C. Russell. *Whiff*. New York: First Quimby Press, 2008.

Carson, Rachel. *Silent Spring*. Boston, MA: Houghton, Miffler, 1962.

Classen, Constance, David Howes and Anthony Synnott. *Aroma*. London: Routledge, 1994.

Corbin, Alain. *The Foul and the Fragrant*, Cambridge, MA: Harvard University Press, 1986.

Curtis, Tony, Williams, David G. *An Introduction to Perfumery*. New York: Micelle Press 2001.

Ellena, Jean-Claude, *Perfume.* New York: Arcade Publishing, 2011.

Firstenburg, Arthur. *The Invisible Rainbow.* Vermont: Chelsea Green Publishing, 2020.

Gattefossé, René Maurice. *Gattefossé's Aromatherapy.* Saffron Walden, UK: C.W. Daniel Company Limited, 1993.

Gilbert, Avery. *What the Nose Knows.* New York: Crown Publishers, 2008.

Huxley, Aldous. *Brave New World Revisited,* New York: Harper & Brothers, 1958.

Lavabre, Marcel. *Aromatherapy Workbook.* Rochester, VT: Healing Arts Press, 1990.

Lawless, Alec. *Artisan Perfumery.* Stroud, Glos: Boronia Souk Ltd., 2009.

Le Guérer, Annick. *Scent.* New York: Turtle Bay Books, 1992.

Loughran, Joni Keim, Ruah Bull. *Aromatherapy Anointing Oils.* Berkeley, CA: Frog, Ltd. 2001.

Louv, Richard. *Last Child in the Woods.* New York: Algonquin Books, 2005.

Lyttelton, Celia. *The Scent Trail.* London: Transworld Publishers, 2007.

McCoy, Anya. *Homemade Perfume.* Salem, MA: Page Street Publishing, 2018.

Patterson, Daniel, Mandy Aftel. *The Art of Flavour.* New York: Riverhead Books, 2017.

Pepe, Tracy. *So, what's all the "Sniff" about?* Brampton ONT: Nose Knows Consulting, 2000.

Pevec, Illène. *Growing a Life.* New York: New Village Press, 2016.

Piesse, G.W. Septimus. *The Art of Perfumery.* Philadelphia, PA: Lindsay and Blakiston, 1867.

Poucher, William Arthur. *Perfumes Cosmetics & Soaps.* London: Chapman & Hall, Ltd., 1929.

Rady, Raed. *The Chemistry of Love.* The Aromatic Thymes, Volume 5.4. 1994.

Rhind, Jennifer Peace. *Listening to Scent.* London: Singing Dragon, 2014.

Robbins, Tom. *Jitterbug Perfume.* New York: Bantam Books, 1984.

Rose, Jeanne, Susan Earle. *The World of Aromatherapy.* Berkeley, CA: Frog, Ltd., 1996.

Rovesti, Paolo. *In Search of Perfumes Los.* Venice: Blow-up, 1980.

Rumi, Jalāl ad-Dīn Muhammad. *Rumi's Little Book of Life.* Newburyport, MA: Hampton Roads Publishing, 2012.

Savinelli, Alfred. *Plants of Power.* Summertown, TN: Native Voices, 2002.

Schnaubelt, Kurt. *Advanced Aromatherapy.* Rochester, VT: Healing Arts Press, 1998.

Schnaubelt, Kurt. *Medical Aromatherapy.* Berkeley, CA: Frog Books, 1999.

Suskind, Patrick. *Perfume.* London: Penguin Books, 1987.

Tisserand, Robert. *The Art of Aromatherapy.* Rochester, VT: Healing Arts Press,1977.

Turin, Luca. *The Secret of Scent.* New York: Harper Collins, 2006.

Turok, Neil. *The Universe Within.* Toronto ONT: Anansi Press, 2012.

Upson, Tim, Susan Andrews. *The Genus Lavandula.* Oregon: Timber Press, 2004.

Wolynn, Mark. *It Didn't Start with You.* New York: Penguin Random House, 2016.

Worwood, Susan. *Essential Aromatherapy.* San Rafael, CA: New World Library, 1995.

Worwood, Valerie Ann. *Aromantics.* London: Bantam Books, 1993.

Worwood, Valerie Ann. *The Complete Book of Aromatherapy and Essential Oils.* San Rafael, CA: New World Library, 1991.

Worwood, Valerie Ann. *The Fragrant Mind.* London: Doubleday, 1995.

Worwood, Valerie Ann. *The Fragrant Heavens.* London: Doubleday, 1999.

Acknowledgements

Each person who supported me in writing this book deserves an armful of roses. I am deeply grateful to Margaret Angus, my number one cheerleader, who encouraged and sustained me and wouldn't let me quit. A huge thank you to each of my early readers and local wordsmiths for their invaluable insight and input: Renée Goff, Patricia Hetherington, Hamilton Jones, Leah Morgan, Elizabeth Neil, Ulrich Schaffer, Elaine Smith and Dorothea Tenute. A heartfelt thanks to the writers in my writing groups over the years for keeping me inspired and on track: Betty Baxter, Heige Boehm, Kim Fenton, Claire Finlayson, Katherine Grunder, Jo Hammond, Del Lobo, Louise McKelvie and Cindy Squazzin.

Without the steadfast guidance of my writing mentor Betty Keller, I wouldn't have a book. I am grateful for having had the honour to work with her. Many thanks to my editor Sheila Cameron for her keen-eye and wisdom, and to Suzanne Doyle-Ingram and Beth Nightingale at Prominence Publishing for their skill and enthusiasm in pulling the many pieces together and getting my book out into the world.

I thank my dear family and good friends for their patience and kindness in bearing with me through the long haul, and the Black Bean Café in lower Gibsons for their lattés, fabulous muffins and the countless hours I spent at the little table by the window. And last but above all, a humble thank you to the Creator who oversees all things.

www.ingramcontent.com/pod-product-compliance
Lightning Source LLC
Chambersburg PA
CBHW021400090426
42742CB00009B/943